CONTENTS

Foreword

by Irene Khan, Secretary General, Amnesty International

I met Jamila, a 16-year-old Afghan girl, in the women's prison in Kabul last year. The prison was full of women accused of adultery, running away from brutal husbands or wanting to marry the man of their choice. Jamila had been abducted from her home in Kunduz a year earlier, forced into marriage, abused and raped. When her husband's uncle threatened to rape her, she could not bear it any longer and ran away. But she was caught by the police and sent to prison for deserting her husband. Jamila told me she wanted to return to her parents, but she was afraid that her father would kill her because, according to him, she has soiled the family honour. If he did not kill her, the man who had forcibly married her certainly would. Her fears are not unfounded. Earlier that year, the Afghan President Hamid Karzai had granted amnesty to about 20 women and girls like her. Some of them were killed by their own families, others have "disappeared". But despite all this, Jamila's eyes lit up with hope as she told me that one day she would get out of prison, marry the man of her choice and live her life in freedom.

I never met Paloma but I heard about her from her mother. Paloma was one of several hundred young women who were murdered in the city of Ciudad Juárez, on the Mexican/US border. Over a period of 10 years, these women were abducted, tortured, raped and killed. The authorities did little to investigate, prosecute or stop the crimes because the victims were poor, powerless women without any political clout. Many had come to Ciudad Juárez to work in the *maquiladoras* – assembly plants set up by multinational companies on the Mexican border to exploit tax breaks and cheap Mexican labour. Young women like Paloma fuelled the global economy in the hopes of gaining from it but instead became victims of globalization. What shone through in this case was the courage of the mothers of the women killed in Ciudad Juárez. They have organized themselves and are agitating for justice. Together with them and others, Amnesty International succeeded in pressurizing the Federal Government of Mexico to intervene in Ciudad Juárez last year in an effort to end the killings.

The stories of Jamila and Paloma are just two examples among millions of the most outrageous human rights scandal of our times: violence against women.

Women in Asia and the Middle East are killed in the name of honour. Girls in West Africa undergo genital mutilation in the name of custom. Migrant and refugee women in western Europe are attacked for not accepting the social mores of their host community. Young girls in southern Africa are raped and infected with HIV/AIDs because the perpetrators believe that sex with virgins will cure them of their disease. And in the richest, most developed countries of the world, women are battered to death by their partners.

Such violence thrives because too many governments turn a blind eye and allow violence against women to occur with impunity. In too many countries, law, policies and practices discriminate against women, denying them equality with men, and making them vulnerable to violence. In too many parts of the world, women are trapped in a cycle of poverty which breeds violence. Too often gender roles and societal structures reinforce the power of men over women's lives and bodies. In too many communities, religious leaders and the media promote roles, attitudes and customs which seek to subordinate and subjugate women. Too often armed groups flout international humanitarian law and use rape as tactic of war to defeat and humiliate the enemy, and too often they get away with it.

The proliferation of small arms, the militarization of many societies and the backlash against human rights in the context of the "war on terror" is only worsening the plight of women.

Human rights are universal – violence against women has made human rights abuse universal. Women from different countries and continents, from diverse religions, cultures and social backgrounds, educated or illiterate, rich or poor, whether living in the midst of war or in times of peace, are bound by a common thread of violence – often at the hands of the state or armed groups, the community or their own family.

The greatest challenge to this scourge has come from individual women and women's groups who have stood up and spoken out, often at cost to their lives. They have organized themselves to demand justice. They have called for their human rights to be respected, protected and fulfilled. Thanks to their efforts, important breakthroughs have been made in terms of international treaties and mechanisms, laws and policies. But these achievements continue to fall dismally short of the real needs because the promises they contain remain just that.

International treaties and mechanisms are only useful if they are implemented properly. Otherwise they are simply hot air. Laws and policies only offer protection if they are respected. Otherwise they are just printed words. Human rights are only real if they provide real equality and equal protection. So, the challenge still remains to bring about change that will make a real difference in the lives of women. That is what women the world over are calling for today.

Through the Stop Violence against Women campaign, Amnesty International is adding its own voice to that call for action. We have worked with a wide range of people inside and outside Amnesty International to design a multi-faceted campaign demanding change at the international, national and local levels through diverse actors and actions.

We will call on leaders, organizations and individuals to publicly pledge to make human rights a reality for all women. We will lobby governments to ratify the UN Convention on the Elimination of all forms of Discrimination against Women and its Optional Protocol without reservations. In some countries we will demand the abolition of laws which discriminate against women and perpetuate violence. In others we will call for the adoption of laws to protect women, and criminalize rape and other forms of sexual violence. We will listen to the voices of women, work with them and support them to organize themselves. We will engage with communities and local authorities to support programs that enable women to live free from violence.

Amnesty International prepares for the launch of its worldwide campaign to Stop Violence against Women by raising the issue at its biennial International Council Meeting in Mexico in August 2003. A giant banner with delegates' handprints is displayed, together with a poster demanding justice for the hundreds of women murdered in the Mexican cities of Ciudad Juárez and Chihuahua.

We will fight for the equal access of women to political power and economic resources. We will challenge religious, social and cultural attitudes that belittle and endanger women. We will campaign to end impunity for violence against women, whether on the battlefield or in the bedroom.

We will seek the solidarity of men. Men also suffer when women are subjected to violence, and many of them are engaged in the movement to denounce and eradicate violence against women.

The purpose of our campaign is not to portray women as victims and stigmatize men as perpetrators; it is to condemn the act of violence itself. That will require all of us to change, not only as organizations and institutions but as individuals.

This campaign is like no other that we have organized before because it calls on each of us to take responsibility. Violence against women will only end when each one of us is ready to make that pledge: not to do it, or permit others to do it, or tolerate it, or rest until it is eradicated.

Violence against women is universal but it is not inevitable. It is in our hands to stop it. We can end violence against women, and we will end it with your support.

© Paula Allen

Celebrating the opening of the first safe house in Kenya to shelter girls threatened with female genital mutilation. Throughout the world, women are claiming the right to live free from the fear of violence and bringing hope to new generations of girls.

Chapter 1. Stop violence against women

"I really don't know what it was that evening that made me decide to call the police, but I always say it was the sight of cleaning up my own blood." Lorraine, a British woman, was regularly beaten by her partner for eight years before telling anybody. "People have asked me why I didn't just leave, but my partner made lots of threats to me which he always carried out. I was very, very frightened of him. So you get to the point where you live with it, it becomes a normal pattern of life, you adapt, you cope, you hide it." In the UK, emergency services receive an average of one call per minute about violence in the family.[1]

Sixteen-year-old Ndambo was raped by three soldiers in a field near Uvira, South-Kivu province, in the war-torn Democratic Republic of the Congo. They shot at her mother when she tried to protect her. Unable to walk after the attack, Ndambo was carried to the hospital. Because she had no money, she received no treatment, and was unable to procure the document proving rape. The UN Office for the Coordination of Humanitarian Affairs estimated that some 5,000 women had been raped in the area between October 2002 and February 2003, an average of 40 a day.

Fifteen schoolgirls were burned to death and dozens of others were injured in a fire at their school in Mecca, Saudi Arabia, on 11 March 2002. Religious police prevented the girls from leaving the building because they were not wearing headscarves and had no male relatives there to receive them. They also reportedly prevented rescuers who were men from entering the premises.

Violence against women is the greatest human rights scandal of our times.

From birth to death, in times of peace as well as war, women face discrimination and violence at the hands of the state, the community and the family. Female infanticide deprives countless women of life itself. Rape and sexual abuse by relatives, other men, security officials or armed combatants are inflicted on millions of girls and women every year. Some forms of violence,

such as forced pregnancies, forced abortions, bride-burning and dowry-related abuses, are unique to women. Others, such as domestic violence – also known as intimate partner abuse, wife-beating and battering – are disproportionately suffered by women. During conflicts, violence against women is often used as a weapon of war, in order to dehumanize the women themselves, or to persecute the community to which they belong.

Violence against women is not confined to any particular political or economic system, but is prevalent in every society in the world and cuts across boundaries of wealth, race and culture. The power structures within society which perpetuate violence against women are deep-rooted and intransigent. The experience or threat of violence inhibits women everywhere from fully exercising and enjoying their human rights.

Women throughout the world have organized to expose and counter violence against women. They have achieved dramatic changes in the landscape of laws, policies and practices. They have brought the violations, which are characteristically hidden from scrutiny, into the public arena. They have established that violence against women demands a response from governments, communities and individuals. Above all, they have challenged the view of women as passive victims of violence. Even in the face of hardship, poverty and repression, women are leading the struggle to prevent violence against women.

A survivor of sexual violence in Sierra Leone, where systematic rape and other forms of sexual violence have been used as weapons of war and to instil terror during a decade of internal conflict.

Initiatives to address and prevent violence against women have proliferated throughout the world in recent years. However, in many countries women's rights activists have been confronted by a renewed mobilization of forces that see gender equality as a threat to social stability and entrenched economic interests. In parts of the world, legal and policy gains by women are being reversed, repealed or ignored. Many governments lack the awareness or the political will to tackle the issue. In the face of deeply imbedded attitudes and interests, local as well as global efforts to eradicate violence against women have progressed in fits and starts.

A human rights scandal

The statistics of violence against women reveal a worldwide human rights catastrophe.

- At least one out of every three women has been beaten, coerced into sex, or otherwise abused in her lifetime, according to a study based on 50 surveys from around the world. Usually, the abuser is a member of her own family or someone known to her.[2]

Violence against women includes, but is not limited to:
- Violence in the family. This includes battering by intimate partners, sexual abuse of female children in the household, dowry-related violence, marital rape and female genital mutilation and other traditional practices harmful to women. Abuse of domestic workers – including involuntary confinement, physical brutality, slavery-like conditions and sexual assault – can also be considered in this category.
- Violence against women in the community. This includes rape, sexual abuse, sexual harassment and assault at work, in educational institutions and elsewhere. Trafficking, forced prostitution and forced labour fall into this category, which also covers rape and other abuses by armed groups.
- Gender-based violence perpetrated or condoned by the state, or by "state actors" – police, prison guards, soldiers, border guards, immigration officials and so on. This includes, for example, rape by government forces during armed conflict, forced sterilization, torture in custody and violence by officials against refugee women.

In any of these categories, violence may be physical, psychological, and sexual. It may be manifested through deprivation or neglect as opposed to overt acts of violence or harassment. These are not mutually exclusive categories. Physical violence by an intimate partner is often accompanied by sexual violence, deprivation, isolation and neglect, as well as by psychological abuse.

- The Council of Europe has stated that domestic violence is the major cause of death and disability for women aged 16 to 44 and accounts for more death and ill-health than cancer or traffic accidents.[3]

- More than 60 million women are "missing" from the world today as a result of sex-selective abortions and female infanticide, according to an estimate by Amartya Sen, the 1998 Nobel Laureate for Economics.[4] China's last census in the year 2000 revealed that the ratio of new-born girls to boys was 100:119. The biological norm is 100:103.

- In the USA, women accounted for 85 per cent of the victims of domestic violence in 1999 (671,110 compared to 120,100 men), according to the UN Special Rapporteur on violence against women.[5]

- The Russian government estimates that 14,000 women were killed by their partners or relatives in 1999, yet the country still has no law specifically addressing domestic violence.[6]

- The World Health Organization has reported that up to 70 per cent of female murder victims are killed by their male partners.[7]

Violence against women is characteristically under-reported because women are ashamed or fear scepticism, disbelief or further violence. In addition, definitions of the forms of violence vary widely in different countries, making

Violence against women: a definition

Amnesty International bases its work on the definition in the UN Declaration on the Elimination of Violence against Women: "any act of gender-based violence that results in, or is likely to result in, physical, sexual or psychological harm or suffering to women, including threats of such acts, coercion or arbitrary deprivation of liberty, whether occurring in public or in private life." (Paragraph 1)

Gender-based violence against women is violence "directed against a woman because she is a woman or that affects women disproportionately".[8] In other words, not all acts which harm a woman are gender-based and not all victims of gender-based violence are female. Some men are victims of gender-based violence, for example, gay men who are harassed, beaten and killed because they do not conform to socially approved views of masculinity.

Progressive interpretations of the definition found in the UN Declaration affirm that acts of omission – such as neglect or deprivation – can constitute violence against women. More recent international legal instruments broaden the definition, in particular to include structural violence – that is, harm resulting from the impact of the organization of the economy on women's lives.[9]

comparisons difficult. Many states lack good reporting systems to determine the prevalence of violence against women. The failure to investigate and expose the true extent of violence allows governments, families and communities to ignore their responsibilities.

Ethnic Albanians leave the woods where they had been hiding for three days to escape the shelling of their villages in Kosovo. Refugees are at risk before, during and after their flight in search of safety. Millions of women around the world have been forced to flee their homes because of violence and conflict.

Roots of violence

The underlying cause of violence against women lies in discrimination which denies women equality with men in all areas of life. Violence is both rooted in discrimination and serves to reinforce discrimination, preventing women from exercising their rights and freedoms on a basis of equality with men.

The UN Declaration on the Elimination of Violence against Women states that violence against women is a "manifestation of historically unequal power

Kuwaiti women seek to register their names as part of their long-running campaign to gain the vote. In early 2003, women were again denied the right to vote in elections. Gender equality is the precondition for the eradication of violence against women.

relations between men and women, which have led to domination over and discrimination against women by men" and that "violence against women is one of the crucial social mechanisms by which women are forced into a subordinate position compared with men".

Despite its pervasiveness, gender-based violence is not "natural" or "inevitable". Violence against women is an expression of historically and culturally specific values and standards. Social and political institutions may foster women's subservience and violence against them. Certain cultural practices and traditions – particularly those related to notions of purity and chastity – may be invoked to explain or excuse such violence.

Although violence against women is universal, many women are targeted for specific forms of violence because of particular aspects of their identity. Race, ethnicity, culture, language, sexual identity, poverty and health (particularly HIV status) are some of the many risk factors for violence against women.

Poverty and marginalization are both causal factors leading to violence against women, and also consequences of violence. The negative effects of globalization are leaving more and more women trapped on the margins of society. It is extremely difficult for women living in poverty to escape abusive situations, to obtain protection and to access the criminal justice system to seek redress. Illiteracy and poverty severely restrict women's ability to organize to fight for change.

Young women are often subject to sexual assault not only because they are women, but also because they are young and vulnerable. In some societies, girls have been subjected to forced sex because of the fallacy that sex with a virgin will cure a man of HIV/AIDS. Recent statistics from studies by UNAIDS have shown that girls in sub-Saharan Africa between the ages of 15 and 19 are six times more likely to be HIV-positive than boys of the same age, in large part due to rape, coercion and the inability to negotiate safer sex practices.[10]

Age provides no protection from violence against women. While some societies respect elderly women's wisdom and afford them greater status and autonomy, others abuse those who are frail and alone, particularly widows. Organizations in Zimbabwe, for example, have recorded an increase in attacks on widows, who are accused of being witches and blamed for the rising rates of HIV/AIDS.[11]

Control of women's sexuality is a powerful means through which men exert their dominance over women. Women who transgress norms of femininity often face severe punishments and have little hope of redress. Men's ability to control women's sexual expression and their reproductive lives is reinforced by the actions or inaction of the state. Violence against women is rooted in discrimination because it denies women equality with men in terms of control over their own bodies and their physical, psychological and mental well-being.

Violence in conflicts devastates the lives of both men and women, but systematic rape, as seen in many recent conflicts, is primarily directed at girls and women. Rape, mutilation and murder of women and girls are common practices of warfare, committed both by government forces and armed groups.

Gender-specific forms of violence are also endemic in militarized or war-torn societies. In societies heavily influenced by gun culture, the ownership and use of arms reinforces existing gender inequalities, strengthening the dominant position of men and maintaining women's subordination. Violent disputes in the home often become more lethal to women and girls when men have guns. In the USA, 51 per cent of female murder victims are shot. In South Africa, more women are shot at home in acts of domestic violence than are shot by strangers on the streets or by intruders.[13]

In September 2002, a 20-year-old Jordanian man was sentenced to just 12 months in prison for the murder of his sister. He had strangled her with a telephone cord when he found out that she had been pregnant when she married her husband. In its ruling, the court decided to reduce the premeditated murder charge to a misdemeanour because the woman had "tarnished her family's honour and reputation."[12]

A six-year-old girl in Santander, Colombia, was raped by two neighbours in 1997. When a local army-backed paramilitary group found out, they killed the two men in front of her, "so that this would never happen again." The girl stopped talking for a long time, because she thought the same thing could happen to her and she felt guilty for the deaths of the men.[14]

A distressed woman in a US shelter for battered women is comforted. Many survivors of violence against women suffer not only physical and psychological damage, but also homelessness, poverty and exclusion.

Long-term damage, widespread harm

The consequences of violence against women go far beyond immediate physical damage to the victim. Psychological damage, and the threat of further violence, erode a woman's self-esteem, inhibiting her ability to defend herself or take action against her abuser. When the violence is unrecognized and unacknowledged, there are further psychological consequences and the woman is less likely to seek help. Some of the long-term effects of violence against women are abuse of alcohol and drugs, depression, other mental health disorders and suicide.

The repercussions of violence against women reverberate throughout the family and community. Studies show that children exposed to violence are more likely to become both victims and perpetrators.[15] In Nicaragua, children who witnessed their father beating their mother were more than twice as likely as other children to have learning, emotional and behavioural problems.[16] Friends and neighbours may also suffer. Recent data from Tokyo, Japan, shows that when restraining orders were violated, relatives and friends who offered victims shelter themselves became targets of the abuser's violent behaviour.[17]

Actual or threatened violence creates a pervasive atmosphere of fear that limits the lives of women, restricting their freedom of movement and their ability to participate in public decision-making and affecting their standard of living.

Violence against women impoverishes society economically, politically and culturally, by limiting the active role that women can make in the development of their community. While it is difficult to determine the full cost to society of violence against women, a growing number of studies point to the serious economic consequences, including loss of productive time, loss of earnings and medical costs. In the developing countries, an estimated five per cent of the working time lost by women because of disability or sickness results from gender-based violence and rape.[18] Research conducted in India estimates that women lost an average of seven working days after each incident of violence.[19] Female victims of domestic violence in Chile lost an estimated US$1.56 billion in earnings in 1996, approximately two per cent of the country's gross national product.[20]

Violence unchecked

As long as the perpetrators of violence against women can commit their crimes without fear of prosecution or punishment, the cycle of violence will never be broken.

Impunity for violence against women is complex – many women are unwilling to pursue intimate partners through the legal system because of emotional attachments and the fear of losing custody of their children. Women are also discouraged from seeking justice through the courts because too often criminal justice systems hold them responsible for violence, asserting that it was "incited" or "instigated" by the woman's own behaviour. Since women are often denied equal access to economic and social rights, many do not have the financial resources to access the legal system.

In some countries, discrimination against women is written into the law. Even where laws are not discriminatory, the actual practices of government agencies, police and prosecutors often foster discrimination and violence against women. Unless a woman can show physical evidence of the violence

Rape and other forms of sexual violence against women and girls characterized 14 years of almost continuous armed conflict in Liberia. In August 2003, around the time of President Charles Taylor's resignation from the government and departure from Liberia, armed opposition forces, government soldiers and militia raped and assaulted large numbers of girls and women. The youngest reported victim was just eight years old.

"That night I called the ambulance, no ambulance came. I called the police, no police came."
Joy struggled through 10 years of brutal violence at the hands of her husband, a police officer in Barbados. In August 2000, her husband tried to kill her with a cement block, and she was only saved by members of his family. Joy's husband is now under a restraining order to prevent him from abusing her.[21]

she has suffered, police and other law enforcement authorities may be unwilling to believe and assist her. Communities may be complicit in excusing or condoning violence against women. They may tacitly approve state failures to bring perpetrators to justice.

Accountability

Grace Patrick Akpan was stopped by police officers for an identity check in Catanzaro, Italy, in February 1996. When she told them that she was an Italian citizen, they answered that "a black woman cannot be an Italian citizen", and described her over the police radio as "a coloured prostitute". She was physically assaulted by the officers and required two weeks' hospital treatment on release. In October 1999, almost three years later, the officers responsible were found guilty of abusing their powers and causing Grace Patrick Akpan injuries. They were sentenced to just two months' probation.

Sometimes government officials or other agents of the state (such as the police, judges, prosecutors, prison guards, security forces, or staff at public hospitals or educational institutions) are directly responsible for committing acts of violence against women.

However, in many cases, the perpetrator is not an agent of the state but a private individual, group of individuals or an organization. Husbands, family members, doctors, religious leaders, the media, bosses and businesses may all be responsible for violence against women. Amnesty International believes that these private (non-state) actors, including economic actors such as businesses, must also respect basic human rights. Everyone has basic duties in relation to human rights.

The human rights community customarily holds governments accountable for their failure to prevent violence against women, and looks to governments to take measures to protect their human rights. While the primary obligation rests with national governments, as part of its strategy to stop violence against women Amnesty International will also identify the roles and responsibilities of a wide range of actors, including parallel legal authorities, local, regional and municipal authorities, and armed groups.

In many countries "parallel" authorities run by clan elders, tribal chiefs or religious leaders exert formal or informal control over women's lives and bear responsibility for violations of women's human rights. Sometimes they commit acts of violence against women; sometimes they encourage or permit such acts. However, in countries where the criminal justice system is ineffective, such authorities may also be – in some cases – the only effective means of providing redress for women who assert their rights.

Power over key rights for women, such as education and social services, often rests with local or municipal authorities rather than national governments. These authorities also have the power to protect women from violence, through the police, courts and shelters. Engaging local authorities in combating violence against women is therefore critical.

Some of the most horrifying accounts of rape, mutilation and murder of women and girls have emerged from recent conflicts across the globe, committed both by government forces and armed groups. One of the goals of Amnesty International's campaign to stop violence against women is to seek an end to impunity not only of governments but also of armed groups for gender-based violence committed by their forces.

Accountability may be particularly difficult to establish when the pattern of abuse crosses national borders. Trafficking of women and girls, the abuse of migrant workers or refugees and the plight of irregular or undocumented migrants raise particular challenges of how to ensure protection and remedies for women for whom no country acknowledges responsibility. Such patterns are confronted with increasing frequency as the effects of globalization impact on women's lives.

Poster from Cambodia

The human rights framework

One of the achievements of women's rights activists has been to demonstrate that violence against women is a human rights violation. This changes the perception of violence against women from a private matter to one of public concern and means that public authorities are required to take action. The parallel development of international and regional human rights standards reinforces this accountability.

> Violence against women is not only a crime, it is also a violation of women's human rights. The description of rape, for example, in some legal codes as an "affront to woman's honour or chastity" is totally inadequate. Rape is a profound violation of a woman's bodily and mental integrity and can be a form of torture, an offence so serious that it is of concern to the entire international community.

Framing violence against women as a human rights issue creates a common language for the work of anti-violence activists and facilitates global and regional networks. These networks are taking their own governments to task, and instigating new international legal standards and practices. The explicit inclusion of rape as a war crime and crime against humanity in the statutes of international criminal tribunals exemplifies these new standards. Such standards signify an increased commitment on the part of the international community to end violence against women and to bring perpetrators to justice.

The human rights framework also specifies governments' obligations under international law to promote and protect women's human rights. It provides mechanisms for holding governments to account if they fail to meet these obligations.

One of the most powerful features of the human rights framework is the core principle that human rights are universal – all people have equal rights by virtue of being human. The appeal to universality counters one of the most common excuses used to justify violence against women, that it is acceptable because it is part of the society's culture. All human rights should be enjoyed by all people, and culture or tradition do not excuse the violation of women's basic human rights. Universality does not impose uniformity or deny diversity. Human rights can be universal only if understood in terms of the rich range of different cultures and experiences.

The struggle to establish women's rights as human rights has been long and difficult. Women's rights are not necessarily prioritized in the agendas of many non-governmental organizations, civil society groups and political parties, which still sometimes fail to recognize them as human rights. Civil society groups are not immune from prevailing social attitudes, and some undoubtedly include men who are themselves perpetrators of violence against women.

Women's human rights activists have to overcome the prejudice against women taking a leadership role in communities or societies which view the woman's role as strictly one of family responsibilities. Women who dare to challenge social and religious conventions have been subjected to public

In the Philippines, women's groups spent several years organizing to bring about a revision in legislation on sexual violence that described rape as a "crime against chastity" under Philippine family law rather than as a violent crime against a person. Under the family law provision, in the case of rape, the woman had to prove that she did not willingly surrender her virginity. The law was finally changed in 1997 and rape was redefined as violence against a person.[22]

© Lizzie Sadin/Editing Server

accusations aimed at discrediting their character. They have been called man-haters, prostitutes, lesbians, unmarriageable, provocateurs or troublemakers.[23] Women protesting against discriminatory laws and practices are often accused of being traitors to their faith or culture or enemies of the state. Women human rights defenders face particular risks when they defend rights that are central to women's integrity, identity and autonomy, such as sexual and reproductive rights.

Despite the risks involved, programs and projects to address, combat and prevent violence against women have flourished over the past decades. An

A man accused of domestic violence is questioned by an examining magistrate in France. Women's rights activists around the world have established that violence against women is not a private issue but demands a response from governments, communities and individuals.

enormous range of anti-violence initiatives now operate in all parts of the world. Some are run by small grass-roots women's groups, others by large international agencies, and still others by governments. Moreover, growing research efforts have resulted in an increasingly detailed and sophisticated understanding of the causes and consequences of violence against women.

Amnesty International's campaign

Amnesty International's campaign to Stop Violence against Women, launched in March 2004, is intended as a contribution to the efforts of women's rights movements around the world.

This report, published for the launch of the campaign, highlights the responsibility of the state, the community and individuals for taking action to end violence against women. It aims to show that women's self-organization, bolstered by the solidarity and support of the human rights movement, is the most effective way to overcome violence against women. Amnesty International's campaign is designed to mobilize both men and women in organizing to counter violence and to use the power and persuasion of the human rights framework in the efforts to stop violence against women.

The human rights movement in general – and Amnesty International is no exception – has been slow to come to the defence of women. It has taken a long time to overcome the false division between violations in the public arena and violations in the private sphere. Since the mid-1990s, Amnesty International has campaigned to establish that women's rights are human rights, but more has to be done to establish gender equity at the heart of Amnesty International's work. This will require increasing awareness of the gender-based aspect of human rights violations, undertaking more research into violence against women and building genuine partnerships with women's movements around the world to combat violence against women.

The Universal Declaration of Human Rights – the foundation stone of the human rights movement – proclaims that all human beings are equally entitled to civil, political, social, economic and cultural rights. With this campaign Amnesty International will show that the right of women to be free from violence is integral to the Universal Declaration. Until violence against women is eradicated, the Universal Declaration of Human Rights will remain unfulfilled.

The solidarity of men is an essential component in Amnesty International's strategy for achieving the eradication of violence against women. Men are not just perpetrators of violence, it affects them and those they love, and many stand up against it. The human rights movement offers men a place in which they can make this stand effectively. Amnesty International is issuing a strong call to men to join the campaign to stop violence against women and will be mobilizing all its members and supporters, men and women, to this end.

Women arrive in Paris at the end of their journey through 23 French cities in 2003. They are carrying a banner reading "neither whores nor submissives" to protest against violence against women and girls in housing projects.

Chapter 2. Sexuality, violence and rights

In Hassi Messaoud, Algeria, an imam at a local mosque reportedly denounced single women living in the area as prostitutes. That night, in July 2001, about 300 men attacked 40 women who lived alone. Many of the women had travelled to the oil-rich region after the breakdown of their marriages and had found work as domestic servants in wealthier neighbourhoods. Their homes were ransacked. Some women reported having their faces slit. Others were burned or stabbed with knives. Almost all reported being sexually assaulted, some were raped and at least three were gang-raped. The imam denied that he had incited violence. Around 40 men were arrested and charged with theft, rape and assault among other crimes. In June 2002, a court acquitted 10 of the men and sentenced the others to up to three years' imprisonment for participating in an illegal gathering and aggravated theft.

This incident illustrates society's fear of independent women, the false presumption that women who have acquired a degree of economic independence are sexually autonomous, and how easily such fears can erupt in violence.

Every human being has the right to physical and mental integrity. This basic human right, guaranteed by international law from the Universal Declaration of Human Rights onwards, means that women and girls have the right to control their own bodies. However, women's freedom to assert this control is all too often restricted by violence and the threat of violence exerted by the state, the community and individuals.

Violence is often used to control women's behaviour, to ensure chastity and the inheritance of property and to maintain the prestige of the family and the society. In order to "protect" women, many societies impose restrictions such as dress codes or curbs on the freedom of movement. Women who challenge these rules are often punished.

Human rights law prohibits all forms of violence against women, physical, psychological and sexual. When a woman is beaten, sexually assaulted or subjected to forced abortion, sterilization or "virginity testing", her right to physical and mental integrity is violated.

Controlling women's behaviour

"The human rights of women include their right to have control over and decide freely and responsibly on matters related to their sexuality, including sexual and reproductive health, free of coercion, discrimination and violence. Equal relationships between women and men in matters of sexual relations and reproduction, including full respect for the integrity of the person, require mutual respect, consent and shared responsibility for sexual behaviour and its consequences."
(Paragraph 96 of the Beijing Platform for Action, the inter-governmental agreement reached at the end of the Fourth UN World Conference on Women)

The control of women's sexuality is central to maintaining the subordination of women. Female genital mutilation is an extreme manifestation of violence used to curtail female sexual expression. Other examples include regulating how women pursue their sexual life; their ability to choose their partners; and whether and when they have children.

"A woman who is perceived to be acting in a manner deemed to be sexually inappropriate by communal standards is liable to be punished...In most communities, the option available to women for sexual activity is confined to marriage with a man from the same community. Women who choose options which are disapproved of by the community, whether to have a sexual relationship with a man in a non-marital relationship, to have such a relationship outside of ethnic, religious or class communities, or to live out their sexuality in ways other than heterosexuality, are often subjected to violence and degrading treatment."
UN Special Rapporteur on violence against women[24]

In many societies, women and girls have no choice as to who they marry. Forced marriages are widespread, despite the provisions of international human rights law that give every woman the right to consensual marriage. In addition, early marriages are common in some countries although marriages of young girls, who are not in a position to give informed consent to sexual relations, violate the UN Convention on the Rights of the Child, a treaty ratified by virtually every country in the world.

In Afghanistan, for example, the practice of forcing girls and young women to marry is widespread. Although forcible and underage marriages are crimes under Afghan law, neither society at large nor the judicial system treat them as a criminal offence. For example, the grandmother of an eight-year-old girl approached a court, seeking proceedings against a 48-year-old man to whom her granddaughter had been forcibly married. Under Afghan law, the legal age for marriage is 16. The court refused to act.

If Afghan girls and women resist forced marriages, they often face criminal punishment. Amnesty International interviewed a number of girls and young women in prison in 2003 whose families had put pressure on the police and courts to imprison them after they had refused to marry. The legal basis for these detentions was, in most cases, unclear. In one case investigated by Amnesty International, a 14-year-old girl, who had been forcibly married by her family at the age of 13 and was reportedly abused by her husband, was sentenced to three years' imprisonment for leaving him. "Running away from home" is a crime in Afghanistan.

Women who have little or no choice but to use their sexuality in order to survive are at risk of human rights violations in many parts of the world. In China, where prostitution is illegal, Amnesty International has documented widespread police abuse of women accused of being prostitutes, many of whom have migrated from the countryside to towns and cities. With alarming frequency, police detain and torture women in order to extract lists of alleged "clients" to blackmail. Many alleged prostitutes and clients have died in custody, while others have committed suicide shortly after being released. These practices are so common that they have come to constitute a major source of income for many police officers.

Despite the taboo on discussing sex and sexuality openly – a taboo with which women's rights activists have to grapple during their campaigning – sex and sexuality are highly politicized. Women's bodies are often used as symbols in political battles. While society attempts to control men's sexuality as well as women's, social strictures are particularly virulent – and violent – when it comes to regulating women's sexuality.

Women who have sex with other women, whether or not they identify themselves as lesbians, have been targeted for

"It is impossible for a woman to complain about forced marriage….If she complains the family will kill her."
A woman interviewed by Amnesty International in Jalalabad, in eastern Afghanistan.

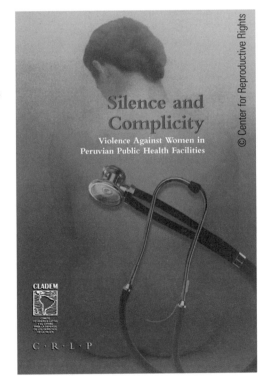
© Center for Reproductive Rights

human rights abuse. Some have been forced into medical treatment or imprisoned in their homes by families that seek to "cure" them of their sexual identity or orientation. According to a non-governmental organization in India, women have reported being given powerful drugs by psychiatrists after being "diagnosed" as lesbian, while others report undergoing "aversion" therapy.[26]

"They locked me in a room and brought him every day to rape me so I would fall pregnant and be forced to marry him. They did this to me until I was pregnant."
The testimony of a young Zimbabwean lesbian whose family locked her up and forced her to submit to being raped by an older man, in order to "correct" her sexual orientation.[27]

Women who contest society's norms of sexuality may also be punished by the state. The International Gay and Lesbian Human Rights Commission reported that a video crew working on a television series on sexuality, sponsored by a Bolivian lesbian organization *Mujeres Creando*, was assaulted by police in La Paz, Bolivia, in August 2002. Actors, crew and activists involved in the project were beaten and kicked, and the police used tear gas to break up a group of bystanders. Twelve crew members were arrested and charged with "obscene acts" and "obscene performance". Subsequently, however, the authorities allowed the crew to continue filming.

One aspect of how women's choices are controlled is through the strict enforcement of a dress code. In some countries cruel, inhuman and degrading punishments are inflicted on women who transgress the dress code. In countries such as Iran and Saudi Arabia, these codes are enforced by the religious police of the state. In others, armed groups attempt to assert their authority by issuing directives regarding "appropriate" dress. Armed groups in

Colombia, for example, told women not to wear skimpy clothing showing their midriffs. Sikh armed opposition groups in the Punjab in India have tried to force women to wear *shalwar kameez* (as opposed to saris or jeans) which they deemed to be Sikh clothing. Just across the border, in Pakistan, Islamist groups deemed the same clothing to be Islamic. In fact, *shalwar kameez*, now worn by many women across South Asia, was originally worn by women of all religions in certain regions in Pakistan and India.

At a conference organized by the network Women Living Under Muslim Laws in 2002, many women from a number of African and Asian countries complained about the spread of the "traditional" headdress which they were increasingly being made to wear. They said that such headscarves were not traditional in their societies, but were being forced on them due to the growing influence of regressive movements over religious institutions and the state. In some countries where secularism is brutally enforced by the state as a mark of "modernity", women are prevented from wearing either traditional forms of dress or more modern expressions of religious political identity. In Turkey, for example, women from Islamist groups have fought to assert their right to cover their heads.

Thousands of women join a lesbian march in Mexico in March 2003. All over the world, women are asserting their right to sexual self-determination despite the widespread use of violence to control women's sexuality.

The notion that women invite sexual violence by the way they dress is widespread. For example, a 2003 government directive in Tanzania banned women civil servants from wearing miniskirts and tight dresses while at work. Politicians in Dar es Salaam claimed that the spread of AIDS would be halted if women stopped wearing short and tight dresses.

This woman was raped at the age of 20 within a relationship. She is a member of the UK-based non-governmental organization Women Against Rape. Rape, a violent crime which can be a form of torture, is greatly under-reported and even more rarely punished.

The Chief Minister of the Malaysian state of Kelantan and leader of an Islamist opposition party, Nik Aziz Nik Mat, commented in September 2003 that "even" women who dressed modestly could "stir up desires" in men by wearing lipstick or perfume.[28] He had previously criticized young women who wore revealing clothes saying that they were inviting men to rape or molest them by their style of dress.[29]

Women and girls are encouraged to wear fashionable, "sexy" clothing by peer pressure, big business, advertising and the media, and yet are held responsible for violence committed against them if they dress "provocatively".

The media sometimes fosters the view that violence against women is acceptable, even sexy. For example, the lyrics of one popular Brazilian song imploring a woman to dance provocatively (*Vai glamorosa*) includes the following refrain:

Se te bota maluquinha
(If you get a bit crazy)
Um tapinha eu vou te dar porque
(I'll give you a little slap because)
Dói, um tapinha não doi, um tapinha não doi
(Hurts, a little slap doesn't hurt, a little slap doesn't hurt)

Sexualized abuse

A significant amount of violence against women takes a sexualized form. In the USA it has been estimated that one in three women will be sexually assaulted in her lifetime.[30]

Rape, a profound violation of a woman's bodily integrity which can be a form of torture, is prevalent throughout the world. However, it is greatly under-reported because of the stigma attached to it, and even more rarely punished. In one country which has particularly high numbers of reported rapes, South Africa, the police have estimated that only one in 35 incidents are actually reported.[31] Estimates from France suggest that out of 25,000 cases of rape committed every year, only 8,000 are reported to the police.[32]

Many women do not consider that they have a right to refuse sex with their husbands and in some countries, laws governing rape do not include marital rape: a woman is presumed to have given permanent consent to intercourse upon getting married. For example, according to section 375 of the Indian Penal Code, "sexual intercourse by a man with his own wife, not being under 15 years of age, is not rape".

Rape as a weapon of war has been seen in conflicts in every region of the world in recent decades, often with an ethnic, religious or political dimension. In Guatemala, during the civil war of the 1970s and 1980s, massacres of Mayan villagers were preceded by the rape of women and girls. In Algeria, hundreds of women were abducted and raped by armed groups in the 1990s. Some were killed during captivity; others managed to escape or were later released. Combatants in recent ethnic-based conflicts in the Balkans and in Central and West Africa used rape and sexual violence to target women of particular ethnic groups and as an instrument of genocide.

Sexualized abuse can also take the form of humiliation – stripping women and parading them naked, simulating sex acts with them or verbal abuse.

A form of state-sanctioned abuse which seeks to control women's sexuality while at the same time violating women's physical integrity is "virginity testing". The forcible examination of the genitalia to look for damage to the hymen involves pain, humiliation, and intimidation and is ineffective as a test for virginity or rape, yet its use continues in countries in various regions including Afghanistan, South Africa and India.[33]

In Turkey, in February 2002, after widespread campaigning by women's groups and human rights groups, the government rescinded a controversial law that allowed schoolgirls suspected of having pre-marital sex to be given "virginity tests". Forced gynaecological examinations had been common under a previous law until five students attempted suicide by taking rat poison rather than be subjected to the test. In January 1999 the Justice Minister ordered a halt to "virginity tests" unless they were ordered by a judge to provide evidence in a criminal case. Research conducted at a hospital in Istanbul after the ban on "virginity testing" found that only 16.8 per cent of the tests were performed for forensic purposes. The rest were conducted for other "social" reasons. Such tests have also allegedly been used to humiliate particular groups of women, such as politically active women in custody in Turkey.

In a high-profile case in Italy in February 1999, the Supreme Court of Appeals in Rome overturned a rape conviction, because, they said, the complainant must have consented to sex because her jeans could not have been removed without her "active collaboration". Women members of Parliament were so outraged at the ruling that they called for a "skirt strike," asking women to wear jeans until the court changed its decision. The Supreme Court referred the case back to an appeal court. In October 1999, a Naples appeal court acquitted the accused man.

Sabina Ngedu Lesirikali was walking home after school near the village of Archers Post, central Kenya, in 1988 when she was reportedly raped by two UK soldiers. Her mother found her unconscious and bleeding under a tree. About a month later Sabina found that she was pregnant. She gave birth to twins, one of whom died when he was three months old. Sabina was left with one child and had to stop going to school. She says that since the rape, she has been regarded as inferior by her community and is not allowed to take part in traditional ceremonies. Her son is often derided by other children and referred to as a "mzungu", a white person. Hundreds of allegations of rape have so far been made against members of the UK army posted to Kenya for training over a period of more than 30 years.

Unfortunately when attempts to protect women from violence are based on the idea that women's sexuality is inherently vulnerable, they can lead to further limitations on women's rights. For example, efforts to counter Bangladeshi women being trafficked abroad where they work as housemaids and nurses have resulted in laws that contravene their freedom of movement.

Reproductive rights

In Katsina state, northern Nigeria, all seven women imprisoned in the women's wing of Katsina Central Prison in early 2003 were held for abortion-related offences. One had been convicted and faces the death penalty on a charge of culpable homicide. Others faced the same capital charge, and two were also charged with aiding and abetting a miscarriage. All the women, who were largely from deprived, rural backgrounds, were unmarried or divorced when they became pregnant, and were reported to the police by village heads, neighbours or other third parties. In none of their cases have the internationally recognized procedures for fair trial been followed.

> **Reproductive rights: a definition**
>
> "Reproductive rights rest on the recognition of the basic right of all couples and individuals to decide freely and responsibly the number, spacing and timing of their children and to have the information and means to do so, and the right to attain the highest standard of sexual and reproductive health. They also include the right of all to make decisions concerning reproduction free of discrimination, coercion and violence." (Cairo Programme for Action, paragraph 7)

Reproductive rights – the right to reproductive health care and the right to reproductive autonomy – are central to women's control over their own lives. Both the International Conference on Population and Development (Cairo 1994) and the Fourth UN World Conference on Women (Beijing 1995) affirmed that reproductive and sexual health are part of fundamental human rights. The declarations from those conferences linked reproductive and sexual health to the personal rights of bodily integrity and security of the person, as well as the social right to the highest attainable standard of health care and the information and the means to access it.[34]

Article 16 of the UN Convention on the Elimination of All Forms of Discrimination against Women (CEDAW) protects women's right to decide on the number and spacing of their children. Yet an estimated one in six women of reproductive age throughout the world undergo unwanted

A woman in Katsina Central Prison, Nigeria, who is facing the death penalty for having an abortion. Under international human rights law, women have the right to decide on the number and spacing of their children.

From three to ninety three, women are raped.

Z
ZERO TOLERANCE

HUSBAND, FATHER, STRANGER – MALE ABUSE OF POWER IS A CRIME

© Zero Tolerance Charitable Trust

pregnancies each year. Of the estimated 190 million pregnancies that occur worldwide each year, 51 million end in abortion, including 21 million in countries where abortion is legally restricted.[35]

Amnesty International takes no position on whether or not women have a right to choose to terminate unwanted pregnancies; there is no generally accepted right to abortion in international human rights law. However, the official bodies that interpret human rights treaties are increasingly indicating support for the position that, where it is legal, abortion should be safe and accessible and further that it should be permitted in cases where pregnancy results from rape.[36] International human rights bodies have also urged states to remove criminal sanctions on abortion; that is, women should not be jailed for having an abortion.[37,38]

There are multiple, overlapping reasons why so many women have unwanted pregnancies. They include lack of information and education about contraception, and lack of access to health care and contraception. An estimated 350 million couples worldwide do not have access to the family planning services they need.[39] Most of all, they include lack of choice for women in marriage, and coercion and violence within and outside marriage. In many societies, men make the decision about whether to use contraception, and what methods to use. Women are often unable to negotiate safer sex practices and condom use even in consensual sexual relations for fear that their partners will respond violently.

Freedom of information on family planning issues has been curtailed in a number of countries as a result of a US government policy widely known as the global gag rule. In January 2001, US President George Bush imposed a restriction on funding from the US Agency for International Development (USAID) for overseas family planning programs. Organizations in receipt of USAID funds are

The UN Commission on Human Rights at its 2003 session adopted a resolution on the right to health which called on all states to:
"protect and promote sexual and reproductive health as integral elements of the right of everyone to the enjoyment of the highest attainable standard of physical and mental health."[40]

prevented from using their own funds to provide abortion services (even where legal), to advocate for changes in abortion laws, or to provide medical information about legal abortion services to their patients. A study conducted by a coalition of reproductive health care organizations documenting the effects of the global gag rule in Ethiopia, Kenya, Zambia and Romania showed that health services have been scaled back and reproductive health clinics had closed, leaving some communities with no health care provider. The study found that the policy also impedes HIV/AIDS prevention efforts.[41]

In some countries, women have been forced to undergo abortions or sterilizations by the state. In 2003 a Chinese woman who applied for asylum in the USA after being forced to undergo two abortions was granted asylum on the basis that she would be forcibly sterilized and imprisoned if she were returned to China. A sterilization order against her was pending when she left China. In Peru, between 1996 and 1998, in response to government imposed sterilization quotas, many women were subjected to sterilization without their informed consent.

Violence against women threatens women's bodily integrity. A woman's right to control her body, including her sexuality and reproduction, is a basic human right. The failure to recognize this right allows for practices that cause harm to women and sometimes privilege power and tradition over individual well-being. Yet in spite of the violence with which women's sexual autonomy is circumscribed, women throughout the world refuse to comply with restrictive social norms and customs. All over the globe they are running projects to support women's right to exercise their sexuality free from discrimination, coercion and violence.

"She told me, 'If you get pregnant again, you will die. You might even die today. So you have to sign this.' I was scared and I signed."
A 22-year-old Roma woman describes how a nurse persuaded her to agree to be sterilized as she lay on a hospital operating table before giving birth. In eastern Slovakia, researchers found a pattern of forced and coerced sterilization of Roma women. In most cases, doctors or nurses gave the women misleading or threatening information in order to make them agree to be sterilized while undergoing caesarean delivery.[42]

A *dalit* woman (a member of a socially and economically marginalized caste) washes her hair. Because of her caste she is not allowed to use the public water supply.

© Giuseppe Benanti

Chapter 3. Culture, community and universality

In every part of the world, women's roles and positions in society are prescribed. One of the key aspects of every culture is the way it defines gender roles. Almost without exception women are assigned to roles which are subservient to those of men. Virtually every culture in the world contains forms of violence against women that are nearly invisible because they are seen as "normal".

Gender and gender roles

Gender refers to the attributes associated with being male and female. Rather than being biologically determined, gender is a set of learned behaviours, shaped by expectations which stem from the idea that certain qualities, behaviours, characteristics, needs and roles are "natural" and desirable for men, while others are "natural" and desirable for women. Gender is a critical element of power and inequality. Women's gender roles are generally accorded less political, economic, social and cultural value than those of men.

Even in countries where laws criminalize violence against women, tolerance of violence may be found at all levels of society. The lack of political will to eradicate violence can be seen, for example, in the failure to establish and fund programs to educate the population, to train government employees and to support measures to protect victims of violence. In Spain, for example, emergency centres, refuges and sheltered apartments are unevenly distributed

The UN Special Rapporteur on violence against women has stated: "violence against women in general, and domestic violence in particular, serve as essential components in societies which oppress women, since violence against women not only derives from but also sustains the dominant gender stereotype and is used to control women in the one space traditionally dominated by women, the home."[43]

across the country, based primarily on the ability of non-governmental organizations to open and operate them. It may be particularly difficult for victims to find support in Spain if they do not have citizenship status.

Personal status laws, family and customary laws may condone violence against women. A number of countries follow obedience and modesty laws that require a wife's submission to her husband and give the husband an explicit or implicit right to discipline his wife. In some countries women are considered to be the property of their fathers or husbands. In parts of Kenya, on the death of her husband, a woman is likely to be "inherited" by his brother or a close relative.

Often, the behaviour of a woman is considered to reflect on her family and community. If a woman is seen to be defying her cultural role, she may be held to have brought shame and dishonour on her family and community. In such circumstances, violence or the threat of violence is used as a means of punishment and control. In the most extreme cases, this can result in permanent disfigurement and even death. So-called "honour" crimes are treated leniently in the legal codes of many countries.

In some cases, culture, custom or honour is used as an excuse for distinctly economic purposes. For example, according to Nafisa Shah, who has extensively researched "honour killings" in Pakistan, "honour killing was punishment for violating the honour codes but the tribes have subverted the custom of killing not for honour but to obtain the compensation that the tribal settlement awards to the aggrieved person."[45]

Community pressures and prejudices

Community values may foster or facilitate violence against women. Women themselves are sometimes complicit in perpetrating violence against other women.

Female genital mutilation (FGM), the removal of part, or all, of the female genitalia, is linked in many countries with rites of passage for women. The operation sometimes results in excessive bleeding, infection, trauma and even death and often leads to later difficulties in intercourse and childbirth. According to the World Health Organization, two million girls each year are put through the terrifying and painful experience.[46] The practice is opposed by women's groups in Africa and elsewhere as a violation of the right to physical and mental integrity. Opponents consider FGM a particularly violent form of controlling the status and sexuality of women. In a survey of the practice of FGM in four African countries (Benin, Gambia, Ghana and Senegal), Amnesty International found that resistance to abolishing the practice is partly based on the considerable revenue it brings to those who perform the operation.[47] Eradicating FGM would not only eliminate the primary source of income for the women who perform the operation, but it would also undermine their status.

Many of the girls who undergo FGM do so under duress, but some may willingly undergo the mutilation in the belief that it will make them a "proper woman". In a similar way, although there is no comparable overt coercion, some women in western countries undergo vaginal surgery, not out of medical necessity, but in order to achieve "sexual enhancement". The pursuit of a culturally imposed ideal of beauty or femininity[48] leads women in Western Europe and North America to take risks with their health, whether through extreme dieting, or plastic surgery which is unnecessary for the maintance of their health.

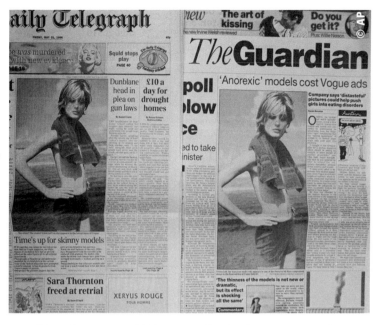

British newspaper headlines in 1996, after a watch-making company withdrew its advertisements from the fashion magazine *Vogue,* claiming that the magazine used models of anorexic proportions. Culturally imposed standards of beauty often lead women to mutilate themselves or damage their health.

Society's image of appropriate gender roles can lead directly to abuse. For example, according to documents gathered by one scholar, promotional material for "mail order brides" is explicit in its message: Filipinas are advertised as having "exceptionally smooth skin and tight vaginas…[they are] low maintenance wives."[49] Women marketed in this way may find themselves subjected to isolation, confinement and violence. Attitudes towards them can range from seeing them as commodities to blaming these women for their fate. Because they often have limited rights to remain in their destination countries, they are often reluctant to contact the police to report cases of abuse.

Cultural stereotypes are often used to justify abuses against women from specific racial, national and religious groups. Amnesty International has identified patterns of racial and ethnic discrimination in gender-based violence in a variety of situations, including abuse of Kurdish women by the police in Turkey and police ill-treatment of immigrant and ethnic minority women in Spain. In far too many such cases, even when perpetrators are found guilty, their sentence does not reflect the gravity of their crime.

Tensions between groups with different religions or cultures are sometimes manipulated for political ends to the point when they erupt into violence. In such cases, women are at particular risk. In the state of Gujarat, India, in early 2002, the ruling Bharatiya Janata Party was reported to have colluded in attacks on the minority Muslim population by Hindu groups. Some groups estimate that more than 250 Muslim women and girls were publicly gang-raped and then burned alive. Many others were stripped naked, raped and mutilated in front of huge crowds but managed to survive. Though large numbers witnessed the rapes, many women have felt too humiliated to disclose what happened to them. As one fact-finding mission explained, "In many ways women have been the central characters in the Gujarat carnage, and their bodies the battleground... Women's bodies have been employed as weapons in this war – either through grotesque image-making or as the site through which to dishonour men, and yet women are being asked to bear all this silently".[50] The state government, administration and police failed to protect these people and in many cases reportedly colluded with the attackers.

Human rights are universal

The universality of human rights has been increasingly challenged by governments and other groups on the grounds that local culture and tradition should take precedence. Cultural relativist arguments are more frequently invoked over issues of gender and sexuality than in any other area within the international human rights movement. These arguments are used to claim that gender-based violence is justified by culture and tradition, despite the fact that cultures are neither static nor unitary. Rather, cultures change and adapt to contemporary circumstances.

According to the UN Special Rapporteur on violence against women, "the greatest challenge to women's rights and the elimination of discriminatory laws and harmful practices comes from the doctrine of cultural relativism" and can only be addressed with the active involvement of the people most affected:
"It is imperative to re-engage and take direction from local people on how women's rights may be promoted in a given context... Without [the local population's] participation and endorsement, no strategy to advance women's rights will succeed. Moreover, any strategy that imposes hard choices from above may only strengthen the polarization in the world today between and within regions."[51]

The meanings of "culture" or "cultural practices" are not singular, nor are they transparent or uncontested. For instance, the government of Pakistan has condemned "honour killings", noting "The practice is carried over from ancient tribal customs which are anti-Islamic". However, Islamic law has been cited in attempts to justify killings in the name of honour. "Culture", "tradition" and "custom" are all open to interpretation by those inside the community.

From a human rights perspective, dissidence and resistance within a culture or community raise questions often inappropriately framed in terms of "collective" versus "individual" rights, with individuals representing the position of dissidence or change. However, what are often described as "culturally

Suklaar, a woman accused of being a witch, sits on the ground in the village of Gambaga, northern Ghana. Gambaga is a so-called "witch village", where women accused of sorcery live after being chased away from their homes.

Women protest in the centre of Madrid, Spain, against domestic violence. The banners read: "Against violence to women" and "Chauvinism is a crime for everybody". Far too often, communities ignore or are indifferent to violence against women in the home.

required restrictions" are, quite frequently, restrictions intended to forestall internal challenges from members of the group. This apparently insoluble "conflict of rights" is often invoked to discredit the entire human rights framework.

The UN Special Rapporteur on violence against women has vigorously tried to counter cultural relativism in matters of sexuality. In her contribution to the 2001 UN World Conference against Racism in Durban, South Africa, she drew attention to lesbian women of colour, whose experience of discrimination is often compounded by racism, sexism and homophobia.[52]

In responding to challenges to universality, human rights activists need to confront the tension between respecting diversity and difference and affirming the universality and indivisibility of rights. Certain principles are absolute: violence against women is never acceptable, whatever the justification offered.

Confronting the 'backlash'

Women's groups have made enormous strides in the fight for equality and freedom from discrimination and violence. However, over the last 20 years, cultural, religious and ethnic movements in many parts of the world have made organized efforts to reverse this progress and to reassert apparently traditional roles. These movements often justify or excuse violence against women in the name of religion, culture, custom and tradition. The religions, cultures and customs in which such movements are based may not be inherently discriminatory towards women, but those advocating an extreme interpretation often justify or excuse violence against women in the name of maintaining social or religious values. Much of women's activism is vilified by them as disrespectful of cultural traditions or demeaning to cultural particularities – whether women speak from within or outside these cultures and communities.

Frequently these movements are described as "fundamentalist", a term that originates in US-based Christian evangelical movements of the early twentieth century.[53] In contemporary usage, it describes political movements that claim to be returning to the true meaning and practice of religion, tradition or custom. Such movements can be found within Christianity, Islam, Judaism and Hinduism, among others.

Laws designed to comply with particular interpretations of religious scripture, or conservative understandings of tradition or custom, often circumscribe women's freedom of movement and expression and prevent women from seeking political or economic independence.

Often, the agendas of "fundamentalist" movements are framed to correct what they understand to be contemporary social ills by recapturing an imagined past envisioned as culturally pure, religiously observant and socially uncontaminated. Although there is a range of views encompassed by these movements, controlling women's behaviour tends to hold a central place, and the fear of women's increased social, economic and political participation tends to be a shared preoccupation. This is the case for groups that represent themselves as being primarily concerned about submission to scriptural texts (the Torah, the Bible, the Qur'an, the Guru Granth Sahib) or about what they consider to be the dignity of a particular national culture.

Christian organizations from the USA have taken issue with the UN Convention on the Elimination of All Forms of Discrimination against Women (CEDAW) and the UN Convention on the Rights of the Child because

Women using an official "writer" to help with their petition to a court in Kabul, Afghanistan. Women victims of crime are denied access to justice in Afghanistan and there are few prosecutions for crimes against women. Cases which reach the criminal justice system usually do so where a woman or girl has the assistance of a male relative or supporter.

they believe that these two international human rights treaties compromise national sovereignty and family privacy, and that they express a radical feminist agenda.[54] They have achieved some successes in international forums, supporting government blocs (including the Vatican and the Organization of the Islamic Conference) that seek to reverse policy commitments toward gender equality and the advancement of women, and to block ratification of these two human rights treaties.

At the March 2003 session of the UN Commission on the Status of Women (47th session), government delegates, for the first time, were unable to come to a consensus on the "agreed conclusions" that result from the intergovernmental gathering. The issue that blocked such a consensus was a disagreement over the language to express the intergovernmental bodies' commitment to ending violence against women. As one observer described it, "Only half an hour before the 15-day session was to end, Iran's representative, supported by delegates from Egypt and Sudan, rose to register his government's objection to paragraph (o), which read: 'Condemn violence against women and refrain from invoking any custom, tradition or religious consideration to avoid their obligations with respect to its elimination.'"[55] (Other states have raised similar objections in other meetings.) The language under question had been crafted over the past 10 years as a consensus formulation, and closely matches similar statements adopted during the UN World Conference on Human Rights (Vienna, 1993), the International Conference on Population and Development (Cairo, 1994) and its fifth year review (New York, 1999), and the Fourth World Conference on Women (Beijing, 1995) and its fifth year review (New York, 2000). In other words, previously agreed statements on ending violence against women were dismissed.

Without a real commitment of political will at the highest levels of government, local, national, regional and international initiatives to end violence against women will continue to face an uphill struggle. Amnesty International calls on political leaders around the world to declare their commitment to eradicating violence against women and fulfilling the Universal Declaration of Human Rights.

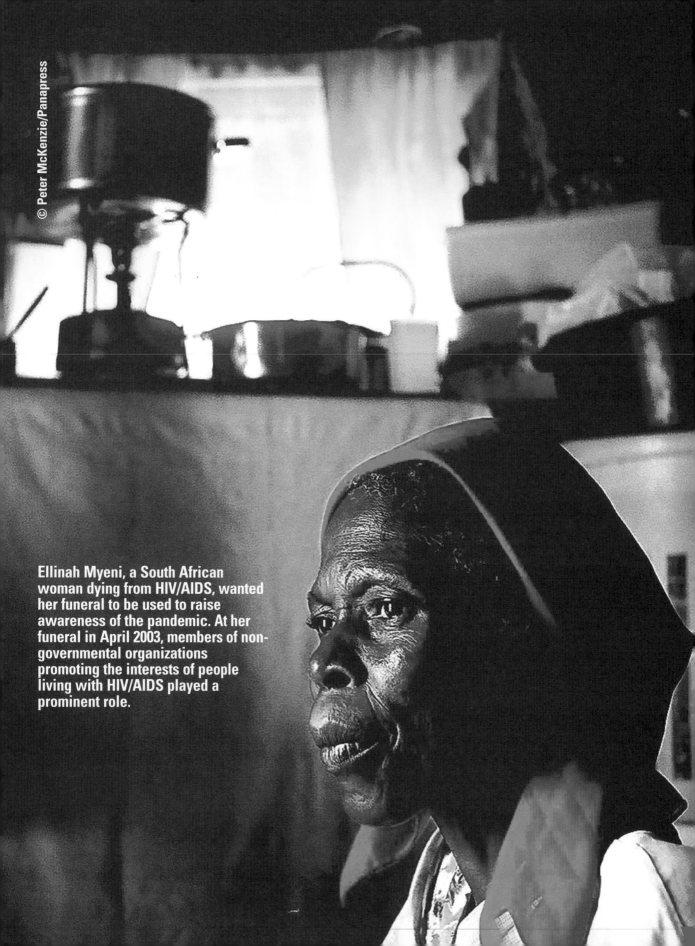

© Peter McKenzie/Panapress

Ellinah Myeni, a South African woman dying from HIV/AIDS, wanted her funeral to be used to raise awareness of the pandemic. At her funeral in April 2003, members of non-governmental organizations promoting the interests of people living with HIV/AIDS played a prominent role.

Chapter 4. Multiple jeopardy – poverty, stigma and discrimination

Violence against women cuts across all class and economic boundaries. However, poverty can be both a cause and a consequence of violence against women. Poverty also exacerbates violence by hampering women's ability to leave violent situations. Worldwide women have a higher incidence of poverty than men; their poverty is more severe than that of men; and increasing numbers of women are poor.[57]

Women face discrimination in access to work, pay and the right to hold property in their own names. Typically women earn and own less than men. Because of the obstacles they face in entering the formal job market, women are more likely to be working in the informal sector, where fewer employment protections apply. They are more likely to engage in unpaid work. As a result, poverty limits the life chances of many women.

Often the gender discrimination that women face is combined with other forms of discrimination, leading to marginalization. Women from racial or ethnic minorities, indigenous women, *dalit* women, lesbian, bisexual and transgender women, women from migrant communities or minority religions, or women who are mentally ill may face such multiple discrimination. The way gender discrimination intersects with other forms of discrimination to produce violence is illustrated by the findings of the Géledés Black Women's Institute, a non-governmental organization based in São Paulo, Brazil.[58] When the organization set up a hotline for women experiencing racial discrimination, most of the calls they received were about sexual abuse and violence against women.

Not only does the damage wrought by violence inhibit women's abilities to earn a good living, but often survivors of violence, particularly sexual violence, are ostracized and excluded. As a result women risk being denied access to health care and the opportunity to support themselves. The nexus of violence, stigma, poverty and marginalization leaves many women and girls permanently at risk and destitute.

"When we, the Afro-women, leave our places of origin fleeing from violence, we think that the war stayed there in our lands, but once in the city we are faced with another war, the war of discrimination over our race, gender and being displaced people… Some displaced Afro-women have not had access to education and they have worked in the fields; when arriving in the city they cannot find a place where they can find work that they know how to do. This situation makes them feel useless, despite the fact that they know how to do many things."
Luz Marina Becerra, a member of the group AFRODES (Association of Displaced Afro-Colombians) in Colombia.[56]

During the 1994 genocide in Rwanda, women were systematically raped and many contracted HIV/AIDS. Only a handful can afford the most effective drugs. Others have been rejected by their families because of the stigma they face as a result of having been raped or having given birth to unwanted children. As their health declines, so does their ability to earn a living. The government has often declared its intention to provide compensation but so far, nearly 10 years on, the promises have proved empty. In dire straits, an increasing number of women and girls engage in "transactional" or "survival" sex, in exchange for money, goods, food, shelter or other gifts.

Entrenched poverty, entrenched violence

Women from all socio-economic groups are at risk of physical, sexual and psychological abuse and deprivation by their intimate partners. However, a recent World Health Organization report suggests that women living in poverty suffer disproportionately.[59]

The common practice of denying women equal rights to property and inheritance exacerbates their subordinate and dependent status. Not only are women denied these economic rights, they are often considered to be the property of their fathers or husbands – as tradeable commodities.

Lack of economic autonomy, denial of property rights or access to housing, and fear of losing their children, means that few women can risk the truly daunting consequences of leaving violent situations and attempting to secure justice from a legal system that may be discriminatory or indifferent.

Victims of violence from marginalized and low-income communities are often denied the level of support that women from wealthier or politically élite communities receive. The UN Special Rapporteur on violence against women, writing shortly after South Africa's first democratic election in 1994, which overturned more than four decades of National Party white minority rule, observed that rape survivors from predominantly white areas in Pretoria and from the impoverished black township of Alexandra near Johannesburg received widely divergent treatment. She noted that the former had access to some police stations which had victim care centres whose facilities helped put the victim at ease and enabled her to tell her story in relative privacy. In contrast, the victim, often of gang-rape, in Alexandra township had to make her report in a crowded, public place at the local police station.[60]

Nearly 10 years after the Special Rapporteur's report, the South African government still faces a huge challenge in providing equal access to good police, medical and legal services for rape survivors. The scale of the problem of sexual violence against women and girls in South Africa is huge: more than 54,000 cases of rape and attempted rape were reported in 2001-2. For the majority of rape survivors living in rural areas or black townships, medical and police facilities are inadequate and over-stretched. The stigma attached to the crime of rape also means the survivor can face brusque and even hostile treatment. Pressures on doctors with excessive workloads can result in perfunctory forensic examinations and inadequate medical histories, to the detriment of the subsequent criminal investigation process. Delays in being seen can also be critical for the health of the rape survivor particularly due to the prevalence of HIV in the population (a national average of 20 per cent) and the risk of transmission as a result of physical trauma to the genitals, especially in child victims.

Non-governmental organizations and women's rights activists in South Africa have long battled to address these problems. In recent years, they have gained significant national and provincial government support for reforms which are gradually helping to improve access to care, treatment and justice for rape survivors. These initiatives include setting up specialized sexual offences courts, victim support centres, and dedicated medical facilities linked more effectively to the police and criminal justice system. The involvement of non-governmental service providers remains critical.

Unequal treatment – women, violence and HIV/AIDS

Women's rights are curtailed by discrimination and poverty both at the local and global level and this places their health and well-being in jeopardy. This conjunction of risk is exacerbated by the effects of the HIV/AIDS pandemic. For example, African women experience disproportionately high rates of HIV/AIDS in a context where their health care needs are restricted both by the unequal global distribution of health care resources and by gender inequality.

The intersection between HIV/AIDS and violence against women, marginalization and poverty is becoming increasingly widely acknowledged.[61] Poverty is both an epidemiological predictor for HIV infection[62] and a growing outcome of the pandemic.

There are many other factors which compound the risks for women.

The link between rape and HIV transmission is well documented and makes women and girls particularly vulnerable. Repeated rape by a partner appears to be a particular risk factor for HIV transmission. The overwhelming majority of rape victims, with the attendant risks of pregnancy and HIV (and other sexually transmitted infections), are women and girls. Preventative drug treatment within 72 hours of exposure is believed to reduce the likelihood of transmission of HIV, but few women in poor countries have access to such treatment.

Violence or the fear of violence inhibits women's capacity to negotiate safer sexual practices, including within marriage. Women attempting to negotiate changes to sexual behaviour with male partners – for example, the use of condoms – may be accused of infidelity or of having the virus. However, a woman's fidelity will not protect her from exposure to the virus from an HIV-positive husband.

© Jenny Matthews/Network Photographers

A Ugandan woman, who was raped in front of her family, gathers leaves outside her home. In many cases, victims of sexual violence are stigmatized and rejected by their communities and even by their own families.

Numerous reports suggest that women living in poverty, including those who have lost male partners to AIDS, or girls who have lost both parents, may come under pressure to seek income by transactional sex[63] or prostitution to support themselves and their families. This in turn exposes them to the risk of HIV.

Women have less access to information about HIV/AIDS than men. A recent analysis of levels of knowledge about HIV/AIDS prevention in 23 developing countries found that levels of knowledge about HIV/AIDS are almost always higher among men than among women.[64]

Sexual abuse in childhood and an early start to sexual activity may contribute to a pattern of risk-taking in later adolescence and adulthood which in turn will increase the young woman's vulnerability to HIV/AIDS.[65]

Gender inequalities are recognized by UNAIDS as one of the challenges of voluntary counselling and testing.[66] A women who identifies herself as HIV-positive may open herself up to violence stemming from the stigma surrounding HIV/AIDS. The example of Gugu Dlamini, who was beaten to death by members of her community in South Africa after revealing her HIV status, is not unique. It is commonly reported that women fear that their husbands will react violently to the revelation of their HIV status.[67]

At present only around 5 per cent of people living with AIDS in the developing world receive appropriate anti-retroviral drugs. This is due to lack of availability, cost and health infrastructural problems. In addition, most people living with HIV/AIDS are not aware of their HIV status or the benefit they would gain from medication.[68]

The uneven and unequal effects of globalization can be clearly seen in access to treatment for HIV/AIDS. Multinational pharmaceutical companies have developed a range of anti-retroviral drugs, but the branded drugs are prohibitively expensive for the world's poor. There have been tough negotiations within the World Trade Organization over the balance between intellectual property rights of drug companies and the rights of the world's poor to life-saving drugs. This has resulted in some concessions and a decision on 30 August 2003 to permit more liberal access to generic drugs.[69] However costs remain relatively high in the poorest countries and development organizations remain critical of the deal.[70]

Some countries have bypassed the control of pharmaceutical companies and developed their own supplies of generic anti-retroviral drugs. In the early 1990s, Brazil undertook a vigorous prevention and treatment campaign and developed affordable generic drugs in state laboratories which could be provided free to people living with HIV/AIDS. From 1996 to 2002, more than 60,000 AIDS cases, 90,000 deaths and 358,000 AIDS-related hospital admissions were averted, according to a recent analysis.[71]

'Less than human'

Stigma – shame or social disgrace – is often deployed in order to portray some groups of people as less deserving or even less than human and is used as an excuse for violence. For example, lesbians and women who do not act as appropriately "feminine" heterosexual women often face stigmatization and violence. Ian Swartz from The Rainbow Project (TRP) in Windhoek, Namibia, which works on behalf of gays and lesbians, reported:

"About 25 per cent of the women who call the TRP hotline are calling to report a rape. They usually don't tell us at first, but in a later conversation, they will disclose being raped… What's worse is that some of their families honestly believe forcing their daughter to have sex will 'fix' them."[72]

Some women become stigmatized as a result of violence, due to the pervasive view that women are responsible for the violence committed against them. Being raped has a devastating impact on the life of the victim. In Afghanistan, for example, loss of virginity is perceived as ruinous to the prospects of women and girls. Commenting after a rape case, one witness told Amnesty International, "What's the point of investigation? Her life is over."

Tens of thousands of women in Bosnia-Herzegovina were raped in the course of the conflict in the region in the early 1990s. Most were Muslim, but Serbian and Croatian women were also victims. According to numerous testimonies, many women were repeatedly raped, became pregnant and were then kept in detention until it was too late to get an abortion. However, rape survivors and the children born of the violence are not considered to be war victims. Rather, as one account describes, "They are regarded as tarnished, at worst as 'fallen women' who somehow invited their own misfortune."[73] This despite the fact that the International Criminal Tribunal for the former Yugoslavia has firmly established rape and sexual enslavement as war crimes and crimes against humanity. The Bosnian non-governmental organization Medica Zenica has recently started an initiative to seek the status of "civilian victim of war" for these women, which may entitle them to state benefits.

Violence at work – exploiting discrimination

Many women face poor working conditions, sexual harassment and violence at work. In most countries, domestic workers work long hours for low pay, sometimes under conditions of involuntary servitude or near enslavement. All too often, the law provides no protection.

Women who organize to challenge the discrimination that condemns them to low pay and dangerous conditions have frequently had to brave harassment and intimidation.

In Guatemala, women trying to gain trade union recognition at *maquilas* (assembly plants owned by multinational corporations) have been abducted, raped and beaten by *maquila* owners and hired gunmen employed by them, some allegedly operating in collusion with members of the security forces. *Maquila* workers, the majority of whom are women, have to work long hours in hazardous conditions; some reported that they were locked inside the factory and forced to remain until they met their daily output quota. They also reported sexual assaults and physical beatings by factory officials.

One of the effects of globalization has been the large numbers of women compelled by poverty and marginalization to leave their homes in search of employment. Uprooted from their communities and social support structures, they are often more vulnerable to exploitation and violence. In the Mexican city of Ciudad Juárez, hundreds of young women have been abducted and murdered with impunity in the past decade. Located on the US/Mexican border – only metres away from the gleaming towers of El Paso, Texas – the city contains a large number of *maquilas* where international companies take advantage of tax benefits and cheap Mexican labour. Despite the low pay, the need for a wage and the proximity of the border has turned Ciudad Juárez into an "attractive" city for a large number of young women from different parts of Mexico. Many of the missing or murdered women were employed in *maquilas*. Waitresses, students and women working in the informal economy have also been targeted.

Women who leave their countries in search of work and a better life are often at grave risk of extreme abuse either by people traffickers or unscrupulous employers. Efforts to report this abuse and escape conditions of involuntary servitude, bonded labour or enslavement are frequently met with indifference by police and border officials. Indeed, the response of authorities to the complaints of victims of trafficking can be further abuse in the form of deportation back to the dangerous or abusive conditions which the women fled. Thus, women who find the courage to leave abusive situations do not always find support for their bravery. For instance, Amnesty International found that women who had been trafficked to Israel and subjected to grave human rights violations were routinely deported without consideration of the conditions to which they were being returned.

A demonstration against unemployment in Germany. Lack of independent financial means can render women vulnerable to violence and limit their chance of pursuing redress.

Migrant domestic workers are frequently ignored by their country of origin and considered unimportant by their country of residence. In Saudi Arabia, despite a labour code that contains a number of provisions that are beneficial for women (such as paid maternity leave and protection from dismissal during pregnancy and maternity leave) domestic workers are

Following an earthquake in Turkey in 1999 the Women's Solidarity Foundation was formed to "provide all women with the means to be independent and stand on their own feet". This group has come together to contribute to this work.

explicitly excluded from protection. In case after case, women migrant domestic workers describe how they are forced to work 18 to 20 hours a day, expected to sleep in corners or corridors, raped with regularity and beaten. In the rare cases when domestic workers are able to make complaints to the police, their claims are ignored, ridiculed or merely denied by their employers and the authorities take no further action or punish the woman herself.

Challenging discrimination and violence

Women who defend the human rights of women, especially women from marginalized racial or ethnic groups, often find themselves to be under threat of violence. Many human rights defenders face risks, but women encounter additional risks because of their gender and the issues they address. Because they often challenge cultural, religious or social norms about the role of women in their society, they are frequently subjected to gender-specific forms of harassment and repression, ranging from verbal abuse to sexual harassment, rape, and murder.

Human rights activists in Guatemala, for example, face daily death threats, attacks and acts of intimidation. Those seeking justice for the atrocities committed during the civil war, in which an estimated 200,000 mostly indigenous people "disappeared" or were killed, are at particular risk, as are those working with indigenous communities.

Despite the risks and difficulties, activists continue to defend women from violence and to confront discrimination. For example, *Puntos de Encuentro*, a foundation based in Managua, Nicaragua, deals with sexuality as a key theme in its media and educational work to promote acceptance of diversity with equity. It has infused its programs with a "popular" approach based on an understanding of human rights that emerges from people's daily lives.

Time after time, women refuse, resist and demand remedies. In housing projects in the suburbs of Paris, France, where many deprived and largely disenfranchised communities live, there have been frequent incidents of sexual violence, including gang-rape, against young women. The response of the women to the violence they face attests to their courage and persistence. Under the slogan "neither whores nor submissives", they have organized marches in their communities and encouraged victims of violence to speak out.[74]

Juana Trinidad Ramírez de Vega, an indigenous Kekchí activist, was killed by an unknown assailant who shot her three times at her home on 5 February 2002 in Libertad Río Dulce, municipality of Livingston, Izabal, Guatemala. Her murder was apparently linked to her work to promote women's health and eradicate violence against women.

Iraqi women walk past a US tank at Al Kadhimiya mosque in Baghdad. After enduring decades of repression and three wars, the women of Iraq now face new hardships, insecurity and increasing restrictions.

Chapter 5. Conflict and violence against women

For women, both peace and war are times of discrimination and violence. Heightened levels of violence are seen in societies which are becoming increasingly militarized, in wars, in countries where conflict is endemic and intergenerational, and in post-conflict situations. In Viet Nam, for example, patterns of domestic abuse from the experience of war are prevalent more than 30 years later. The form, circumstances and extent of violence varies, but there is a continuum between violence in conflict and violence in peacetime.

Militarization

Militarization has been defined as a process whereby military values, ideology and patterns of behaviour achieve a dominating influence on the political, social, economic and external affairs of a society. Violence is not a by-product of militarization but one of its central features, and increased violence in society tends to lead to increased levels of gender-based violence against women.

Militarization is a growing reality in societies all over the world, seen in the use of force to resolve international and internal disputes, foreign occupation, internal conflicts and the proliferation of arms. The global arms trade is both a manifestation of this trend and a contributory factor to increased conflict and aggression. This trade has rapidly expanded over the past few decades. Global military expenditures in the early 1990s were more than 60 per cent higher in real terms than in the 1970s and twice as high as in the 1960s.[75] World military expenditure in 2001 was estimated at $839 billion, a world average of $137 per person. Over the three-year period 1998–2001, it increased by around seven per cent in real terms.[76] In the Beijing Platform for Action, states committed themselves to reduce excessive military expenditure and control the availability of armaments, so as to permit the possible allocation of additional funds for social and economic development, in particular for the advancement of women.[77]

> "Readily available and easy to use, small arms and light weapons have been the primary or sole tools of violence in almost every conflict dealt with by the United Nations. In the hands of irregular troops operating with scant respect for international and humanitarian law, these weapons have taken a heavy toll of human lives, with women and children accounting for nearly 80% of the casualties..."
> UN Secretary-General[78]

The Brazilian non-governmental organization Viva Rio launched a campaign under the slogan Arma Não! Ela Ou Eu (Choose gun-free! It's your weapon or me) to bring together women from all sections of Brazilian society to force the men of Brazil to give up their guns. In June 2001, Viva Rio, the International Action Network on Small Arms and other local groups collaborated with the state government to destroy 100,000 weapons which had been seized by the police – the largest weapons stockpile to be destroyed anywhere in the world on a single day. A further 10,000 weapons were destroyed on 9 July 2002 and Viva Rio has campaigned to have 9 July made Small Arms Destruction Day throughout the world.

Much of the armed violence that affects women, both in and out of conflict, is committed with small arms: guns that can be carried and used by one person. There are approximately 639 million small arms in the world today – one for every 10 people on the planet – and eight million new ones are manufactured every year.[79] Amnesty International is part of a campaign with Oxfam and other non-governmental organizations calling for a new international Arms Trade Treaty to stop the proliferation of all weapons, and for community safety measures to make people safe from armed violence in their everyday lives.

Violence in war

Instability and armed conflict lead to an increase in all forms of violence, including genocide, rape and sexual violence. During conflicts, violence against women is often used as a weapon of war, in order to dehumanize the women themselves, or to persecute the community to which they belong. Women are likely to form the greatest proportion of the adult civilian population killed in war and targeted for abuse. Women and children are also usually the majority of refugees and internally displaced people forced to flee their homes because of armed conflict.

The wars in Bosnia-Herzegovina and Rwanda in the 1990s drew public attention to the horrific levels of violence against women committed in conflict. Murder, systematic and widespread rape and other forms of sexual violence were used not only to destroy the morale of the enemy, but also literally to decimate them. In Rwanda, for example, gang-rape, sexual mutilation and sexual humiliation (for example, making Tutsi women parade naked in public) were prevalent in the genocide.

Women may be targeted for violence because of their roles as community activists and leaders, or those of male relatives. During the Indonesian occupation of East Timor from 1975-1999, women suspected of sympathizing with the pro-independence armed opposition or being related to its members were subject to sexual violence. During a hearing of the Commission on Reception, Truth and Reconciliation in Timor-Leste, former Governor Mario Carrascalao testified about the common practice by the Indonesian military of holding dance parties where young Timorese women were forced to entertain the soldiers.[80] He also stated that wives of armed opposition combatants were forced into sexual slavery by the Indonesian military.

In Nepal, two young girl cousins were abducted by army personnel in April 2002 and were alleged to have been repeatedly raped. The soldiers were pursuing the father of one of the girls who had escaped to India.

During the period following the 1991 military coup in Haiti, a number of women were raped because they or their husbands were political organizers.[81]

In the conflict between the Sri Lankan security forces and the Liberation Tigers of Tamil Eelam (known as the "Tamil Tigers"), women in custody have been blindfolded, beaten, and raped by army, police and navy officials. For example, in March 2001, Sinnathamby Sivamany and Ehamparam Wijikala, two young Tamil women, were arrested by members of the navy in the coastal city of Mannar and taken to the office of a special police unit. Ehamparam Wijikala was brutally raped by two officers inside the police station. Sinnathamby Sivamany was blindfolded, undressed and raped in a van outside the station. Later, both women were forced to parade naked and then suspended for about 90 minutes by their hands and legs from a pole placed between two tables. They were also pinched and beaten with a thick wire.

In the long-running conflict in Myanmar (Burma), Amnesty International has reported numerous cases of rape and killings by the security forces of ethnic minority women. In October 1997, Nang Pang, a 28-year-old Shan woman, was raped by two soldiers. When she said she would tell their captain, a lieutenant kicked her in the chest and threatened to kill her. Her brother-in-law took her to Thailand in December 1997 in order to get medical treatment, but she died in January 1998 because he could not afford to pay for surgery.

Of course, men and boys are also victims of violence in war. In recent conflicts, civilian men and boys have been separated out in towns and villages and then killed, raped, forcibly conscripted, or made to commit acts of violence against women. However, in cases where men, rather than women, are disproportionately targeted, whether as combatants or civilian victims, women constitute the majority of displaced populations and face new problems as a result.

Violence in conflict, violence in the home

Women living through conflict not only have to endure assaults or the threat of assault by the other side, but they also face increased levels of violence from within their families, at the same time as they are depended upon to rebuild their communities from the ground up.

Since the *intifada*, Palestinian women have been exposed to increased levels of violence – not only through the destruction of their homes and communities by Israeli forces, but also through increased domestic violence. A poll conducted by the Palestinian Center for Public Opinion in 2002 showed that "86 per cent of respondents said violence against women had significantly or somewhat increased as a result of changing political, economic and social conditions of Palestinian women," up 22 percentage points from the previous year.[82]

After the war, the violence continues

Violence does not necessarily reduce once the conflict has abated. In the USA, domestic violence and murder by soldiers returning from combat is emerging as a serious issue. One study, conducted by the US Army, found the incidence of "severe aggression" against spouses was reportedly three times as high in army families as in civilian ones.[83]

The World Health Organization notes that "in many countries that have suffered violent conflict, the rates of interpersonal violence remain high even after the cessation of hostilities – among other reasons because of the way violence has become more socially acceptable and the availability of weapons."[84] A study in Northern Ireland showed that the increased availability of guns meant that more dangerous forms of violence were used against women in the home.[85]

Iraqi women have suffered severe hardship for decades: loss of male relatives in the 1980-1988 Iran-Iraq war; mass expulsions to Iran of entire families declared by the authorities to be of "Iranian descent"; government repression, including the chemical weapons attack on Halabja in 1988; the 1991 Gulf War and the subsequent suppression of the Shi'a uprising; 13 years of UN sanctions from 1990 to 2003; and the US-led military action in 2003.

Under the government of Saddam Hussein, women were arbitrarily arrested, tortured, "disappeared" and executed by the authorities on political grounds. In 2000, hundreds of women were said to have been beheaded in public by the paramilitary group *Feda'iyye Saddam*, accused of prostitution.

After the US-led invasion and occupation of Iraq in 2003, during which an unknown number of civilians were killed, the sudden political and security vacuum led to widespread looting and gun crime, and growing reports that women were afraid to leave their homes because of rapes and abductions. However, their homes are not necessarily safe either. The following case was documented by an Amnesty International researcher in Baghdad.

Under the name Women in Black, women in many countries have opposed war and conflict through silent demonstrations. They have also sought to expose the link between conflict and increased violence against women. Here women in Belgrade, Serbia, call for an end to the occupation of Iraq.

Nineteen-year-old Fatima (not her real name) was shot in the legs by her husband in front of his family and their neighbours on 21 May 2003. Fatima was married to her husband at the age of 12 and was treated as a servant and regularly beaten in her husband's family home. On the day she was shot she had tried to run away to her own family, but they sent her back. According to Fatima, when her husband came, "He was very angry and he took his Kalashnikov… I could not believe that he would shoot, his sister was standing beside him…But then he didn't stop, he shot my legs, I could not feel them, they were numb, the sun was setting, I was looking at the sky, I said to the men 'I don't want to die'. They took me to the hospital."

Despite the number of eye-witnesses and the seriousness of the crime, her husband was not arrested.

Research by the non-governmental organization Medica Zenica in Bosnia-Herzegovina showed that 24 per cent of the women interviewed had experienced domestic violence over a long period of time, dating from before the war.[86] The majority also reported that the incidence and intensity of violence increased after the end of the war in 1996. Although it is difficult to ascertain the real level of increase, many groups report "shockingly high percentages of violence against women and children". Social stigma and a lack of services are exacerbated by a criminal code that distinguishes between "an 'assault' and 'light bodily injury committed by a spouse or cohabitant'. In the case of the latter, the victim must bring a prosecution against the perpetrator. The state typically doesn't intervene."[87]

A recently identified trend in post-conflict societies is a rise in violence against women associated with the presence of international peacekeeping forces. For example, women have been trafficked into Kosovo for forced prostitution since the deployment of an international peacekeeping force (KFOR) and the establishment of a UN civilian administration (UNMIK) in 1999. They come from countries including Moldova, Ukraine and Bulgaria, and the majority are reportedly trafficked through Serbia. Trafficking was identified as a problem soon after UNMIK's arrival, but the number of premises where women believed to have been trafficked are forced to work as prostitutes has continued to rise, reaching more than 200 by July 2003.

In a report on trafficking of women and girls to post-conflict Bosnia-Herzegovina, Human Rights Watch gave convincing evidence of the direct responsibility of local police in trafficking – as bar owners and as employees of establishments holding trafficked women and girls. Local police also reportedly received bribes and free services, and tipped off owners about planned police raids, among other forms of complicity and participation. The report also shows the involvement of the UN police monitoring force and the NATO-led peacekeeping troops in trafficking, as clients, purchasers of women, and in retaliation against whistle-blowers.[88]

Other peacekeeping troops have committed acts of violence against women in the communities they are charged with protecting. For example, a sergeant from the Third Parachute Battalion of Belgium stationed in Somalia in 1993 allegedly procured a teenage Somali girl as a birthday present for a paratrooper. She was reportedly forced to perform a strip show at the birthday party and to have sexual relations with two Belgian paratroopers. In 1998 a military court sentenced the sergeant to 12 months' imprisonment, six of them suspended, a fine, and exclusion from the army. Italian troops were also found to have committed sexual violence while stationed in Somalia on the peacekeeping mission in 1993-4. An Italian government commission found credible evidence of a number of instances of gang-rape, sexual assault and theft with violence. There were also reports of sexual violence committed by Italian peacekeeping troops in Mozambique in 1994.

Too often, violence against women is relegated to the sidelines of peace and conflict resolution processes. Moreover, peace processes have routinely failed to include women and to deal with gender issues, which can result in gender-based persecution and violence being rendered invisible in peace agreements and not taken into account in their interpretation and implementation. For example, an Amnesty International delegation which visited Sierra Leone in 2000 reported that the process of disarmament, demobilization and reintegration of former combatants was failing to address the experiences of the many girls and women who had been abducted by rebel soldiers and forced to become their sexual partners. It appeared that when they

© Jenny Matthews/Network Photographers

A camp for people who have suffered deliberate amputations during the conflict in Sierra Leone, where armed opposition forces undertook a deliberate and systematic campaign of mutilations. In the most dire of circumstances, women find the strength to support each other.

reported for disarmament and demobilization, they were often not interviewed separately from their "husbands" and not offered a genuine opportunity to leave, if they wished to do so. These women and girls, many either pregnant or with young children, required support to either return to their families where possible or to re-establish their lives together with their children.

Abuses by armed groups

There are many different – and passionate – views on whether and when it is legitimate to use violence to achieve change or to confront state power. Amnesty International takes no position on this issue – we do insist, however, that groups which resort to force respect minimum standards of international humanitarian law, justice and humanity. Armed groups, no less than governments, must never target civilians, take hostages, or practise torture or cruel treatment, and they must ensure respect for basic human rights and freedoms in territory they control.

Common Article 3 of the Geneva Conventions applies in all cases of armed conflict, and to all parties to the conflict. More detailed rules may apply to armed groups where the conflict reaches a certain threshold of gravity, so that Additional Protocol II to the Geneva Conventions (covering non-international armed conflicts) applies. As a matter of customary law (law which is binding on all states, whether or not they are bound by treaty law), basic human rights norms (directed for the most part at states) might apply to armed groups where they exercise de facto control over territory and take on responsibilities analogous to a government. Indeed, in a number of situations armed groups have expressly indicated their commitment to human rights principles. In any case, individual members of an armed group can be held criminally responsible at an international level for war crimes and crimes against humanity.

Although international legal rules extend to armed groups, in practice these rules have had little impact. Over the past several years armed groups operating in all regions of the world have been responsible for some of the worst human rights abuses, including brutal and systematic acts of violence against women.

Armed groups tend to operate either in opposition to state power, or in situations where state power is weak or absent. In either case, in practice the state in the territory affected cannot be expected to address – in a fair and effective way – the human rights abuses these groups commit. While this poses particular challenges, it does not mean that armed groups are beyond accountability. They need and depend on support, resources and finance from other states, private organizations and sympathetic communities abroad and all of these can wield considerable control over armed groups. The international tribunals for the former Yugoslavia and Rwanda have successfully prosecuted leading members of armed groups and the establishment of the International Criminal Court opens new avenues for pursuing international criminal prosecutions. Human rights advocates all over the world are seeking ways to pressure and engage armed groups to respect human rights, and these efforts must be strengthened. As part of these efforts, greater attention must be given to ensuring that armed groups respect women's basic rights, and discipline forces under their command responsible for violence against women.

Armed groups: a definition

One definition of armed political groups is "groups that are armed and use force to achieve their objectives and are not under state control" (International Council on Human Rights Policy). Other terms used to describe such groups are armed opposition groups, non-state entities, and non-governmental entities. The political nature of such groups is usually used to distinguish them from criminal organizations, like the Mafia. In today's conflicts, however, it is increasingly difficult to separate criminal from political purposes, whatever the group's professed aim. Some armed groups operate with the explicit or tacit support or approval of the state, for example as paramilitary forces, and it is important that states not be allowed to shirk their responsibility to bring such forces under control.

In many parts of Afghanistan, security and legitimate government have not been established since the fall of the Taleban regime in November 2001. In this power vacuum, armed groups have abducted, raped and abused women and girls with impunity. Incidents reported to Amnesty International include the rape of four girls by members of an armed group. The youngest, aged 12, was unconscious due to her injuries when brought to hospital by her parents.

Armed groups frequently use rape and other forms of sexual violence as part of a strategy to instil terror. In Sierra Leone, during a decade of conflict, armed opposition forces undertook a deliberate campaign of mutilation. Civilians had limbs amputated or the letters RUF (initials of the armed opposition Revolutionary United Front) carved into their flesh. Abduction of girls and women, rape and sexual slavery were systematic and widespread. Most victims had sexually transmitted diseases and many became pregnant. Abortion is illegal in Sierra Leone, leaving such women with few options. A 14-year-old sex worker told UNIFEM (the UN Development Fund for Women) that she would have terminated her pregnancy but did not have enough money to pay for it. The cost of an "underground" abortion was $100, "more than the average annual income of most Sierra Leoneans and more money than the girl had seen throughout her whole life."[89]

During the rebel incursion into Freetown in January 1999, rebel combatants went from home to home collecting girls. Those who were not selected to be the "wife" of a rebel commander were repeatedly raped by other rebel combatants. On 8 January 1999 in the Cline Town area in the east of Freetown, a rebel commander ordered that all girls who were virgins report for a physical examination by a woman colleague. Those confirmed to be virgins were ordered to report each night to the rebel commander and other combatants, who raped and sexually abused them.

In some cases, armed groups want to make certain that their victims know who is responsible for their torment. In others, confusion serves as a convenient mechanism for committing acts of violence and escaping responsibility.

Members of armed groups, as well as governments, have a legal responsibility under the basic principles and rules of international humanitarian law to respect the rights of civilians not to suffer violence of any kind, including torture and inhuman or degrading treatment.

Women combatants

The armed forces of many countries include women, sometimes as front-line combatants. Women are not only victims of violence in war, they are sometimes also perpetrators. Approximately 3,000 of those currently imprisoned in Rwanda accused of participating in the 1994 genocide are women. Most are young, with children, and stand accused of participating in the mobs that killed more than 800,000 Tutsis.[90]

Sometimes women are abducted at gunpoint by armed groups and forced to serve as combatants or in other capacities, as has been well documented in Sierra Leone, for example. Other women join armed groups because of their commitment to the group's political goals and ideology. In Sri Lanka, the Liberation Tigers of Tamil Eelam have recruited many young Tamil girls, known as "Freedom Birds".[91] In Nepal, the Communist Party of Nepal (Maoist) is conducting a "people's war", and enjoys considerable support among women, the unemployed, people belonging to traditional "lower" castes, marginalized ethnic groups and poor people in rural areas.

Situations of crisis, displacement, poverty and marginalization make fertile ground for recruitment. One Afro-Colombian woman speaking at a women's meeting in Colombia explained, "The young men and women, upon seeing that

there was nothing to do, go to the mountains and now you see that girls at twelve-years-old want to take up arms…Some will go because they saw their families killed, their parents, and many of them have seen this happen right in front of them."[92]

As the UN Special Rapporteur on violence against women found during her mission to Colombia in 2001,

> "For some girls, the male-oriented culture affects their attraction to uniforms, weapons and the power they represent. Girls often join an armed group thinking that, once they are a part of it, they will be treated as equals and be given the same rights as men. They seek to overcome the exclusion and disregard life in their own families, where they can only be associated with domestic roles."[93]

Female Tamil Tiger fighters in training in northern Sri Lanka in November 2002. Women are not only victims of violence in war, they can also be perpetrators. Voluntarily or under duress, they have fought alongside men in government forces and armed groups.

A woman in Côte d'Ivoire whose house has been destroyed in the conflict which erupted in September 2002. Countless women around the world have been rendered homeless or displaced by conflict and face new dangers as a result.

Despite their search for greater freedom and autonomy, girls and young women who join armed groups often find themselves sexually exploited. Often they are forced into taking contraception or into abortion. One young women testified in Bogotá, Colombia, in July 2001, "When I had just arrived, like within 20 days, they told me that they had to give me an injection and then I said no, I didn't want to… Then the female doctor told me that I had to let them give me the injection …they gave it to me, each month."[94] Another woman described how she was forced to have an abortion by the armed group to which she belonged. When she asked to keep the baby,

> "they said no – just imagine a pregnant bitch in combat or whatever, and with that big belly!...They made me have an abortion...The doctors that scraped me were guerrilla doctors and I was in recovery for two months. Then they had me on watch duty and helping out making meals...I got better. But you aren't the same and you get really hurt."[95]

Other problems faced by women combatants include their treatment if detained – they are often a minority held among male prisoners of war.

In some cases, economic deprivation pushes women into the control of men in armed groups. Amnesty International has reported on the devastating impact of the exploitation of the mineral coltan in eastern Democratic Republic of the Congo by armed groups, foreign armies and their business partners. Women who carry and crush the coltan rock suffer respiratory and reproductive problems. There are also reports of an increase in stillbirths and deformities among these women.[96] An Amnesty International delegation found that impoverished families give their daughters to the "coltan men", to take with them into the mines, in exchange for money or goods.

Fleeing violence, finding violence

Women refugees and asylum-seekers often find themselves caught in an inescapable cycle of violence. Fleeing from one dangerous situation, they may find themselves in an equally hazardous one, vulnerable to violence and exploitation. Many refugees, especially women, are abused during their flight in search of safety. Government officials such as border guards, smugglers, pirates, members of armed groups, even other refugees, have all been known to abuse refugee women in transit. Patterns of violence in refugee settings may reflect those prevailing in the situation they have fled, including the day-to-day violence experienced by women in their homes.

In refugee and displaced camps, the upheaval and feelings of loss of purpose, not least for men, add to the pressures on uprooted individuals and communities. Community structures which might otherwise accord women a measure of protection break down. On the other hand, tensions already present in a family or community, or new tensions, can be exacerbated by the abrupt loss of a social and economic context. The resulting pressures have a detrimental impact on both men and women, and in many cases this leads to an increase in sexual and domestic violence against women.

Serious deficiencies in justice systems, a prevailing climate of impunity and insecurity, and a lack of independent access to registration mechanisms, food distribution systems, and leadership structures combine to expose women to a heightened risk of sexual abuse and exploitation. Women and girls are sometimes not even safe from sexual and other exploitation by humanitarian aid workers – the very people charged with responsibility for the welfare of refugees and the displaced. Such exploitation of women and girls is in many cases symptomatic of the protracted uncertainty which refugees often face. They may live for years in situations where traditional roles or poorly administered humanitarian assistance may perpetuate or worsen social inequality and vulnerability.

Reports in 2002 by the Office of the UN High Commissioner for Refugees (UNHCR) together with Save the Children-UK documented serious allegations of sexual abuse and exploitation of women and children by humanitarian workers in camps for refugees and displaced people in Sierra Leone, Liberia and Guinea. Allegations included humanitarian workers deliberately withholding food and services in order to extort sexual favours. In Nepal, it was acknowledged by UNHCR that Bhutanese refugees in camps were found, in at least 18 cases, to have been victims of sexual abuse and exploitation by refugee aid workers. The victims included a seven-year-old girl and a woman with disabilities.

It is now widely accepted that aid workers must be held accountable for their conduct, and a number of agencies and organizations have issued codes of conduct for staff.

In cities and towns, many refugees scratch a meagre living and live in squalid conditions. Sexual and domestic violence is rife. Sometimes women living illegally in urban areas are forced to pay police officers or other government officials "sexual bribes".

Women and girls who are seeking asylum often face a lack of understanding about the circumstances they have fled and how those experiences affect women. In presenting their claims for protection, they may encounter disbelief or seemingly insurmountable administrative obstacles.

In a number of countries, asylum-seekers are detained in regular prisons where they are effectively treated as criminals. Even in countries where asylum-seekers are detained separately from prisoners, their experience of detention can have a traumatic effect, prompting flashbacks of past torture and suffering. Amnesty International and other human rights organizations have documented incidents of abuse of women and girl refugees and asylum-

The US-based Women's Commission for Refugee Women and Children recounts the following story of what happened to a Ugandan woman who suffered an emotional breakdown while incarcerated in an INS (US Immigration and Naturalization Service) facility in York County, Pennsylvania. "The prison deemed [her] breakdown a suicide attempt and sent in a 'quick response team'. The team consisted of four men, three of whom were wearing riot gear. They also brought dogs…The men, without the presence of a female guard, stripped [her]. She begged them not to remove her bra and panties…they placed her naked and spread-eagled in four-point restraints on a cot."[97]

seekers in detention and conditions which amount to cruel, inhuman or degrading treatment. Women have been humiliated, raped, and in some instances driven to attempt suicide or commit acts of self-harm.

When women return to their countries of origin, they may encounter the perpetrators of the abuses that forced them to flee. Sometimes they find themselves living alongside the perpetrators who are now neighbours or who hold positions of power or influence in the community.

Returning from exile, women and girls may also encounter a whole new set of problems. The breakdown of community structures and traditional roles that often results from conflict and flight presents new challenges in a post-conflict society. In some cases, women in exile have acquired education hitherto denied them, or skills and training opportunities previously not permitted. Reintegration into the society they left behind may expose women and girls to new risks and vulnerabilities.

In December 2001, the UN High Commissioner for Refugees made five commitments to refugee women. They included: ensuring the participation of refugee women in all management and leadership committees; registering refugee women on an individual basis, and providing relevant documentation; developing strategies to counter sexual and gender-based violence; and ensuring direct participation of refugee women in the management and distribution of food. In October 2003, the Executive Committee of UNHCR adopted a *Conclusion on Protection from Sexual Abuse and Exploitation* highlighting the need for measures to empower women in refugee situations, codes of conduct, prompt investigation of allegations of sexual abuse and exploitation, and the need for accountability mechanisms. The Conclusion also recognizes that states, UNHCR and other implementing and operational partners all have the responsibility to take concrete measures to prevent and respond to sexual and gender-based violence. These are important steps to break the cycle of violence to which displaced women and girls are too often exposed. Amnesty International also urges that monitoring, complaints and redress mechanisms should be independent and should be available both in camps and in urban areas.

Women demanding rights and seeking peace

UN Security Council Resolution 1325 reaffirms women's rights to protection in conflict and the need for all parties to armed conflict to take special measures to that effect; expresses willingness on the part of the Security Council to incorporate a gender perspective into peacekeeping operations; calls on all actors involved in negotiating and implementing peace agreements to adopt a gender perspective; and urges member states to ensure increased representation of women at all decision-making levels in national, regional and international mechanisms for the prevention, management and resolution of conflict.

Since the first coordinated international effort to bring women together to organize for peace at the International Congress of Women in 1919, women have organized to resist violence and oppose war. Women have assembled peace missions, crossed battle lines between warring factions, lobbied decision-makers and created global peace initiatives. In doing so, they have demanded justice and asserted their right to participate in peace negotiations.

In 2000, these efforts achieved global recognition when the UN Security Council passed Resolution 1325, which reaffirmed women's right to protection in conflict and post-conflict situations, and also urged increased participation by women in all peace processes. Such participation is critical to ensuring that peace-building and conflict resolution processes are founded on the principles of equality and non-discrimination that are so central to eradicating violence against women.

The adoption of Resolution 1325 resulted from pressure from the women's movement and some of the elected members of the Security Council – notably Namibia, Jamaica and Bangladesh – as well as from UNIFEM and women's and human rights organizations, including Amnesty International. The resolution is widely used as an advocacy tool in international and national arenas, including by women involved in peace processes in post-conflict situations such as Afghanistan, Iraq and Liberia.

In a ground-breaking initiative to involve women in formal peace negotiations, a gender sub-committee was formed in Sri Lanka in early 2003 to advise the main negotiating team on the effective inclusion of gender issues in the peace process. Both the government and the armed opposition LTTE nominated members.

The Women's Caucus for Gender Justice, along with other non-governmental organizations including Amnesty International, campaigned for the inclusion of gender perspectives in the process of setting up the International Criminal Court, a court with jurisdiction over genocide, crimes against humanity and war crimes which can act when national courts are unable or unwilling to do so. They also campaigned for the Court to protect and promote gender justice. The result was not only the inclusion of forms of gender-based violence as war crimes and crimes against humanity in the Rome Statute establishing the International Criminal Court, but also the creation of a Victim and Witness Unit. This unit provides protection to witnesses, and also attempts to prevent victims of violence from being traumatized again in the court procedures.

The non-governmental Urgent Action Fund for Women's Human Rights gives grants to women human rights defenders in crisis situations.

At the grass-roots level, women have braved ridicule and danger in order to assert their opposition to conflict. Under the broad rubric of the name Women in Black, women in a variety of countries have opposed the violence and hatred produced by war through silent demonstrations and have drawn attention to the link between violence in conflict and the continuum of violence against women. Women in Black groups have included Palestinian and Israeli women in Jerusalem and women in Belgrade, Serbia, along with a multitude of supporters worldwide.

Somebody's Life Everybody's Business: Stop Violence Against Women

FIJI WOMEN'S CRISIS CENTRE
88 Gordon St, Suva. PO Box 12882, Suva, Fiji.
Phone: (679) 313300 Fax: (679) 313650

© Fiji Women's Crisis Centre

In the most tense and polarized situations, women still find ways to work across conflict. In Jerusalem, the Jerusalem Center for Women and Bat Shalom were established simultaneously out of an ongoing dialogue between Palestinian and Israeli women. They operate independently but are linked through their coordinating body, Jerusalem Link. Despite the stresses on the relationship between the two organizations, the groups have continued to communicate and work together toward creating an "authentic and effective women's leadership initiative".

South Korean women used as sex slaves by the Japanese Imperial Army during the Second World War demand compensation and redress.

Chapter 6. International human rights law and violence against women

Sustained campaigning by women's rights activists over the past decades has brought significant advances in the commitment of the international community to scrutinize and combat violations of women's rights. The **Universal Declaration of Human Rights** – proclaimed in 1948 by the General Assembly of the UN and still the cornerstone of the UN's human rights system – states that everyone should enjoy human rights without discrimination. The UN Charter affirms the equal rights of women and men. However, "gender blindness" has meant in practice that gross violations of women's human rights have often been ignored and structural discrimination against women not challenged.

Historically, many interpretations of human rights law have drawn stark distinctions between the "public sphere" – political, legal, and social institutions – and the "private" sphere of the home and family, and have only offered protection from abuse in the "public" realm. Doctrines of privacy and protection of the family, found both in international and national laws, have been used to reinforce this artificial divide. Progress in establishing that all forms of violence against women, wherever they take place, can constitute a violation of human rights for which the state can be held accountable, is a major achievement of women's human rights activists.

Using international human rights law as a framework for addressing violence against women presents a methodology for determining government obligations to promote and protect the human rights of women. It also points to the mechanisms available for holding governments to account if they fail to meet those obligations.

Human rights treaties are contracts between particular states that are part of the international community of nations. They also provide guarantees of freedoms and entitlements that individuals ought to be able to claim at the national and, frequently, international level. These treaties set out the obligations that states undertake when they ratify (agree to be bound by) the treaty in question. In general terms, when states ratify a human rights treaty, they agree to: promote the rights in the treaty; secure those rights for all and translate them into policies and strategies; prevent violations of the rights under the treaty; and provide remedies to the victims should their rights be violated. These obligations apply to acts by individuals who operate on behalf of the state, at its instigation or with its consent or acquiescence.

The UN **Convention on the Elimination of All Forms of Discrimination against Women** (CEDAW) expressly requires states parties (those governments that have agreed to bind themselves to the Convention) to "take all appropriate measures to eliminate discrimination against women by any person, organization or enterprise" (Article 2(e)).

Violence as a form of discrimination

The Universal Declaration of Human Rights, which recognizes the human rights which are fundamental to the dignity and development of every human being, states that everyone should enjoy human rights without discrimination on grounds of sex. The UN Charter affirms that the "equal rights of men and women", "the dignity and worth of the human person" and the realization of fundamental human rights are among the UN's core principles and objectives.[98] International human rights treaties and standards define the obligations of states to secure human rights for individuals within their territory and subject to their jurisdiction "without distinction of any kind". The right not to be discriminated against is so fundamental that it is one of the rights that cannot be set aside (derogated from) under any circumstances.

Human rights standards

The detailed mandate to secure equality between women and men and to prohibit discrimination against women is set out in CEDAW. This mandate finds its source in core human rights documents – the Universal Declaration of Human Rights; the International Covenant on Economic, Social and Cultural Rights; and the International Covenant on Civil and Political Rights (ICCPR). The principles in these three documents, collectively known as the International Bill of Human Rights, proclaim the rights to equality, liberty and security and the rights to be free from discrimination, torture, and degrading and inhuman treatment. The International Convention on the Elimination of All Forms of Racial Discrimination and the UN Convention on the Rights of the Child, along with CEDAW, build on the overarching framework of human rights norms and standards by focusing on particular groups.

While these human rights standards lay the foundation for women's right to be free from violence, this was crystallized in 1992 when the Committee on the Elimination of Discrimination against Women adopted **General Recommendation No. 19** on "violence against women."[99] General Recommendation No. 19 defines violence against women as a form of discrimination, and notes that:

> "Gender-based violence, which impairs or nullifies the enjoyment by women of human rights and fundamental freedoms under general international law or under human rights conventions, is discrimination....These rights and freedoms include: a) the right to life; b) the right not to be subject to torture or to cruel, inhuman or degrading treatment or punishment; c) the right to equal protection according to humanitarian norms in time of international or internal armed conflict; d) the right to liberty and security of person; e) the right to equal protection of the law; f) the right to equality in the family; g) the right to the highest standard attainable of physical and mental health; h) the right to just and favourable conditions of work."

General Recommendation No. 19 specifies the nature of governments' obligation to take comprehensive action to combat violence against women. It notes that it applies specifically to violence perpetrated by public authorities, but emphasizes that governments are responsible for eliminating discrimination against women by any person, organization or enterprise (paragraph 9), and that governments are required to prevent violations of rights by any actor, punish these acts and provide compensation (paragraph 9).

In 1993, the UN World Conference on Human Rights in Vienna provided an opportunity for a burgeoning global network of anti-violence activists – the Global Campaign for Women's Human Rights – to achieve policy change among governments at the UN level. There, as a result of an extensive lobby of women's human rights activists, the UN declared violence against women to be a human rights violation, requiring urgent and immediate attention, and proclaimed that women's rights are human rights. Soon after, in December 1993, the UN **Declaration on the Elimination of Violence against Women** was adopted, setting out the mandate for addressing violence against women as a human rights issue.

UN world conferences have, in the past few decades, been an important venue for women's groups to come together across national, regional and identity boundaries to construct common agendas. Regional and global

Women celebrate at the UN to mark the establishment of the International Criminal Court in 2002. In large part thanks to lobbying by women's rights activists, the Rome Statute of the International Criminal Court explicitly recognizes rape and other forms of sexual violence as crimes against humanity and as war crimes.

women's networks have facilitated these endeavours, and provided the opportunity for vastly differing groups of women to lobby in coalition.

One of the most significant outcomes of such lobbying by women in non-governmental organizations and in government delegations is the far-reaching **Beijing Declaration and Platform for Action**, agreed at the Fourth World Conference on Women in 1995. The Beijing Platform for Action (and its five-year review in 2000) has been augmented by agreements from a series of other UN world conferences held in the 1990s and into the 21st century.[100] These agreements allow a more precise identification of the steps that must be taken, by governments and civil society alike, to prevent violence, protect women and girls, and provide redress to victims. While the Beijing Platform for Action is not a treaty, it can be read as a companion piece to General Recommendation No. 19, which fills in many of the details of state obligations grounded in treaty law.

The **Rome Statute of the International Criminal Court**, finalized in 1998, has been a significant development in addressing crimes of violence against women. Several forms of violence against women, including rape, were included in the Rome Statute as war crimes and crimes against humanity. In addition, gender-based persecution was included as a crime against humanity. The draft Elements of Crimes outlines gender-sensitive definitions of crimes[101] and the Rome Statute contains progressive provisions relating to the participation and protection of victims and witnesses in the process, and ultimately for reparation to victims. It also contains progressive provisions relating to women's participation in the International Criminal Court as judges, prosecutors and staff.

A recent addition to the range of international mechanisms with which to oppose violence against women is the UN Convention against Transnational Organized Crime. Adopted in 2000, it has an appended Protocol to Prevent, Suppress and Punish Trafficking in Persons, Especially Women and Children. This Convention and its Protocol define trafficking to include "at a minimum, the exploitation of the prostitution of others or other forms of sexual exploitation, forced labour or services, slavery or practices similar to slavery, servitude or the removal of organs."

There are also regional treaties and agreements which have been drafted and adopted by governments. Regional treaties, such as the **Inter-American Convention on the Prevention, Punishment and Eradication of Violence against Women**, known as the **Convention of Belém do Pará**, are binding on those countries that have ratified them.[102] The Convention of Belém do Pará recognizes that every woman has the right to be free from violence in both public and private spheres. States parties to the treaty commit themselves to condemn all forms of violence against women and agree to pursue policies to prevent, punish and eradicate such violence. A number of cases relating to violations of the Convention of Belém do Pará have been decided by the Inter-American Commission on Human Rights.

In July 2003, the African Union (formerly the Organization of African Unity) adopted its own regional treaty relating to the human rights of women – the **Protocol to the African Charter on Human and Peoples' Rights on the Rights of Women in Africa**. This protocol requires states parties to take measures to suppress all forms of violence against women, identify the causes, punish the perpetrators, and ensure effective rehabilitation and reparation for victims.

A variety of other regional, sub-regional and bilateral agreements aim to make progress toward the eradication of violence against women, or particular forms of violence.

A Brazilian woman was left paralysed after years of domestic violence by her husband. After 17 years, the case against him had not been resolved. In 2001 the Inter-American Commission on Human Rights used both the American Convention on Human Rights and the Convention of Belém do Pará in establishing the nature of Brazil's obligations to apply due diligence to investigate, prosecute and punish domestic violence. The Commission found that the pattern of impunity prevailing in domestic violence cases, and in this case in particular, stood in direct opposition to the state's duties under Article 7 of the Convention of Belém do Pará.[103]

The work of the **UN Special Rapporteur on violence against women** has deepened the international community's understanding of the causes and manifestations of violence against women throughout the world. In addition, the mandates of other UN Special Rapporteurs have increasingly included an explicit commitment to addressing the gender dimensions of the area being covered. This applies both to those reviewing human rights abuses in particular countries and those examining particular issues, such as the right to the highest attainable standard of health, the right to education and the right to housing.

States' obligations

States are required under international human rights law to "respect, protect, and fulfil" human rights. First, states are required to **respect** rights. In other words, government officials, or those acting with the authorization of the state, must not commit acts of violence against women. They must respect the human rights of women to be free from violence by ensuring that no state actors commit acts of violence against women. When a prison guard fondles or hits a woman prisoner, or a male police officer strip searches a female suspect, or a state employed doctor conducts a "virginity test" on a young woman, the state has failed in its duty to respect the human rights of women.

States must also **protect** women's rights. The duty to protect requires that the state and its agents must take effective measures to prevent other individuals or groups (including private enterprises and corporations) from violating the integrity, freedom of action, or other human rights of the individual. This duty is upheld when the state institutes laws, policies, and practices that protect victims of violence, provide them with appropriate remedies, and bring the perpetrators to justice. General Recommendation No. 19 issued by the CEDAW Committee (the expert committee that monitors state compliance with CEDAW) stresses that "States parties should take appropriate and effective measures to overcome all forms of gender-based violence, whether by public or private act."

Finally, they must also **fulfil** these rights, by ensuring the appropriate infrastructure to support these laws, policies and practices, and to render them effective. Moreover, states are expected to report on the progress of laws and policies designed to eliminate discrimination and violence against women and to modify features that are ineffective. States parties to CEDAW and other treaties are required to submit a report every four years documenting their efforts to combat discrimination and eradicate violence. Increasingly, other human rights treaty bodies, such as the Human Rights Committee, which monitors states' implementation of the ICCPR, are integrating gender into their mainstream work, particularly when considering states parties' reports on how they have implemented human rights.[104]

In other words, states are under an obligation to take effective steps to end violence against women. Under this obligation, states must not only ensure that their agents do not commit acts of violence against women, they must also take effective steps to prevent and punish such acts by private actors. If a state fails to act diligently to prevent violence against women – from whatever source – or fails to investigate and punish such violence after it occurs, the state can itself be held responsible for the violation. This is known as the standard of due diligence (see below). This does not absolve the actual perpetrators and their accomplices from being prosecuted and punished for the initial acts of violence.

States must take a comprehensive approach to eliminating **all** forms of violence against women and adopting measures designed to eradicate all forms of violence and discrimination. States have an ongoing obligation to monitor the situation and respond accordingly, changing – or supplementing – tactics when progress subsides.

The recent adoption of an **Optional Protocol** to CEDAW has strengthened the apparatus with which violence against women can be opposed. The Optional Protocol offers women a direct means for seeking redress at the international level for violations of their rights under CEDAW. It is a mechanism that allows victims of violations or those acting on their behalf (including non-governmental organizations) to make a complaint directly to the CEDAW Committee when all domestic avenues of redress have been exhausted or are ineffective (unless such a process will be unreasonably prolonged or unlikely to bring effective relief). It also allows the CEDAW Committee to undertake investigations of systematic abuses. As of September 2003, 75 states had signed the Optional Protocol, and 55 had ratified or acceded to it.

Many of the states that have ratified CEDAW have entered reservations to it. A reservation is a legal objection to a particular clause or article in a treaty which a state otherwise agrees to be bound by. Reservations which are "incompatible with the object and purpose of the treaty"[105] are prohibited. The effect of reservations is to weaken states' commitment to upholding the rights in the treaty, particularly by reducing their obligation to change their domestic laws. There are many reservations to CEDAW on the issue of the general commitment to implementing equality between men and women, and specifically in relation to family and nationality law. These impact on women victims of violence, as difficulties in obtaining divorce, custody of their children, or a passport, will affect their ability to leave abusive situations.

A study on the impact of CEDAW found that it was an important instrument in advocacy by non-governmental organizations and in their dialogues with government officials. Change requires action at many levels, and often faces stiff resistance, but the study found clear examples of progress. In Japan, for example, the ratification of CEDAW in 1985 had a major impact: an Equal Employment Opportunity Law was enacted, and subsequently amended to prohibit discrimination against women in recruitment and promotion, and the Labour Standards Law was reformed to benefit women. In Turkey, long-term efforts by the women's movement at many level of society to obtain legislation against domestic violence (the Family Protection Law) were boosted by dialogue between the CEDAW Committee and Turkish officials. In Ukraine, CEDAW principles were included in a new constitution adopted in 1998. In Nepal, several key non-governmental organizations have used CEDAW in their lobbying and campaigning, and two bills to address violence against women have been presented to Parliament.[106]

Due diligence

The concept of **due diligence**[107] describes the degree of effort which a state must undertake to implement rights in practice. It is particularly valuable in assessing the accountability of governments for the acts of private individuals and groups. States are required to make sure that the rights recognized under human rights law are made a reality in practice. In addition, if a right is violated, the state must restore the right violated as far as is possible and provide appropriate compensation. The standard of due diligence is applied in order to assess whether they have carried out these obligations.

According to the UN Declaration on the Elimination of Violence against Women, states should "exercise due diligence to prevent, investigate and, in accordance with national legislation, punish acts of violence against women, whether those acts are perpetrated by the state or by private persons." The standard of due diligence has also been implicitly incorporated into the Convention of Belém do Pará (Article 7b).

A range of measures is open to a state to ensure that the rights of women and men are respected; the specific course of action is to be determined within the context of each country, in view of its particular political, economic, religious, cultural and social institutions. However, social and cultural practices may not be used to justify or excuse inaction or inadequate measures on the part of the state. In fact, Article 5 of CEDAW specifically calls upon states parties to "modify the social and cultural patterns of conduct of men and women, with a view to achieving the elimination of prejudices and customary and all other practices which are based on the idea of the inferiority or the superiority of either of the sexes or on stereotyped roles for men and women."

Equal protection of the law

Human rights law is based on principles of equality and the right to be free from discrimination. State responsibility to address abuses of women's rights also arises from state obligations to ensure that all those subject to their jurisdiction receive equal protection of the law. Under international law, states must ensure protection of human rights to all, without discrimination.

States that discriminate in the protection of human rights on a number of specified grounds commit a human rights violation. For example, Article 2 of the ICCPR obliges states parties to ensure the rights in the Covenant to all in their jurisdiction, without discrimination on various grounds, including sex. Article 3 of the ICCPR emphasizes this, specifying that states parties must ensure the equal right of men and women in the enjoyment of all the rights set forth in the Covenant, such as the right to life (Article 6) and the right not to be subjected to torture or cruel, inhuman or degrading treatment (Article 7).

The ICCPR also states, "all persons shall be equal before the courts and tribunals" (Article 14). Women victims of violence have a right to the enforcement and the protection of the law equal to that of any other victim of violence; if states fail to ensure this, such discriminatory treatment on grounds of gender violates the right to equal protection of the law.

Freedom from torture

The right to be free from torture and cruel and inhuman treatment is fundamental to allowing an individual to live a life of dignity and security. The ICCPR requires that states "ensure" freedom from torture or ill-treatment. However, torture of women is routine in states in every region of the world. In the definition of torture set out in the UN Convention against Torture and Other Cruel, Inhuman or Degrading Treatment or Punishment

(Convention against Torture), one of the expressly prohibited purposes of torture is discrimination.

Article 1 of the Convention against Torture defines state responsibility for acts of torture and ill-treatment by private individuals (such as abusive husbands or other family members) if carried out with the "consent or acquiescence of a public official". Human rights experts have pointed out that all the elements of torture can be present in domestic violence (violence in the family). It may cause severe physical and mental pain, and may be intentionally inflicted for a specific purpose. If a state tacitly condones domestic violence by not exercising due diligence and equal protection in preventing and punishing it, then it bears responsibility for the abuses.

Rape as torture

International human rights courts and international criminal tribunals have affirmed that the pain and suffering caused by rape are consistent with the definition of torture. In many circumstances under international law, rape has been acknowledged as a form of torture owing to the severe mental and physical pain and suffering that is inflicted on the victim. Not every case of rape, however, engages the responsibility of the state under international law. The state is accountable under international human rights law for rape by its agents. It is also accountable for rape by private individuals when it has failed to act with due diligence to prevent, punish or redress it.

Amnesty International's recent worldwide campaigns against torture have included a focus on women and on torture and ill-treatment based on sexual identity. *Broken bodies, shattered minds: Torture and ill-treatment of women*[108] puts the case that acts of violence against women in the home or community constitute torture for which the state is accountable when they are of the nature and severity of torture and the state has failed to fulfil its obligation to provide effective protection. *Crimes of hate, conspiracy of silence: torture and ill-treatment based on sexual identity*[109] notes that the prevalence of sexism and homophobia in societies puts lesbians at grave risk of abuse in the home and in the community.

International law and armed conflict

International humanitarian law (including the Geneva Conventions and their Additional Protocols) applies to the conduct of all parties to armed conflicts, whether international or internal. The international human rights framework can also apply to the actions of the state and its security forces during periods of armed conflict. In all cases, the state is accountable for the actions of armed groups that work in association with it or are tolerated by it (such as paramilitary forces, militias, death squads or vigilantes). Members of armed groups, whether allied to the state or not, are required, as a minimum, to respect the provisions of Article 3 common to all four Geneva Conventions and to refrain from violence to civilians, including murder, torture and inhuman treatment of all kinds, including rape and other forms of sexual violence. They are also liable under international criminal law for committing war crimes (including breaches of common Article 3) and crimes against humanity.

Acts of violence against women in conflict are prohibited under both international human rights and humanitarian law. Under customary international law (law which is binding on all states, whether or not they are bound by treaty law), many acts of violence against women committed by parties to a conflict constitute torture. In addition, the following acts are war crimes: rape, sexual slavery, enforced prostitution, forced pregnancy, enforced sterilization and certain other forms of sexual violence of comparable severity. If these acts are knowingly committed as part of a widespread or systematic attack on a civilian population, they constitute crimes against humanity.

Torture of women in an international armed conflict is a war crime under the Geneva Conventions, and, in certain circumstances, may constitute an element of genocide. Acts of violence against women amounting to torture, war crimes, crimes against humanity and genocide are subject to universal jurisdiction. This means that under international law, the authorities in any country where people suspected of such crimes are found can – and should – investigate, regardless of where the crime was committed. If there is sufficient admissible evidence, that

state should prosecute the suspects, extradite them to a state able and willing to do so in a fair trial without the death penalty, or surrender the suspects to an international criminal court.

In the 1990s, a public outcry ensued when women were detained and repeatedly raped in conflicts in the former Yugoslavia and Rwanda. Since then, the creation of the International Criminal Tribunals for the former Yugoslavia and Rwanda and the new International Criminal Court have greatly increased the capacity of the international legal system to address violence against women in conflicts. These tribunals provide the means for holding those most responsible (state or non-state actors) accountable for crimes such as genocide, crimes against humanity, and war crimes.

Jean-Paul Akayesu, a former mayor, outside the International Criminal Tribunal for Rwanda. In 1998 the Tribunal convicted him of genocide and crimes against humanity. Rwandan women testified that he had not intervened to stop repeated mass rape and murder by the militia, despite his power to do so. This unprecedented judgment recognized that rape and sexual violence could constitute genocide and provided a definition of rape under international law.

In the first judgment by an international court for rape and sexual violence as genocide, on 2 October 1998, the International Criminal Tribunal for Rwanda convicted Jean-Paul Akayesu, a former mayor, of genocide and crimes against humanity and sentenced him to three life terms. Rwandan women testified that he had not intervened to stop repeated mass rape and murder by the militia, despite his power to do so. His sentence also included 80 years for rape and encouraging pervasive sexual violence. This unprecedented judgment recognized that rape and sexual violence constituted genocide "if committed with the specific intent of destroying, in whole or in part, a particular targeted group." It also provides a definition of rape under international law as a physical invasion of a sexual nature, committed on a person under circumstances which are coercive.

The International Criminal Tribunal for the former Yugoslavia convicted two Bosnian Muslims and a Bosnian Croat of war crimes which included the rape of Bosnian Serb women. Witnesses at the Čelebići trial[110] described how camp inmates were tortured, beaten to death by guards wielding baseball bats, set on fire, and raped. At the Foca trial,[111] three Bosnian Serb commanders were accused of forcing Muslim women into sexual slavery. In a February 2001 judgment, the Tribunal firmly established that rape is a crime under customary international law, and handed down the first ever conviction for rape and enslavement as crimes against humanity.

In large part thanks to extensive lobbying by women's rights and human rights activists, the Rome Statute of the International Criminal Court recognizes rape and other forms of sexual violence as crimes against humanity and as war crimes. The crime of rape applies to situations in which a woman provides sex to avoid harm, to obtain the necessities of life, or for other reasons that have effectively deprived her of her ability to consent. Trafficking is encompassed within the crime against humanity of enslavement. Also, for the first time, gender-based persecution is included as a crime against humanity. The codification of these crimes in the Rome Statute is a significant step in combating impunity for perpetrators of grave violence against women in conflict.

Right to international protection

Women flee their homes for a wide variety of reasons including persecution, war, natural disasters, violence and poverty. Some seek asylum in another country, others try to find safety elsewhere in their country of origin. Some go to refugee camps or to camps for the internally displaced within their own countries. If they reach another country, the reason for their flight will determine whether or not they are considered refugees under international law, and therefore entitled to international protection.

The internationally applicable definition of a refugee is set out in the 1951 Convention relating to the Status of Refugees and its 1967 Protocol (the Refugee Convention). Rights under the Refugee Convention apply not only to refugees in individual asylum systems, but also to refugees in situations of mass influx, where tens or hundreds of thousands of refugees may cross a border in a matter of days.

A growing number of countries in recent years have granted asylum to women on the grounds that certain acts of violence against women, including in some cases domestic violence, may be considered sufficiently serious to constitute a form of harm amounting to persecution within the meaning of the Refugee Convention (as amended by the 1967 Protocol). Gender can influence or even determine both the type of harm perpetrated and the reasons for it. Women have been granted asylum because of the risk that they would be subject to female genital mutilation, domestic violence, and other forms of serious gender-related harm. In some cases, they have suffered persecution because they are lesbians, have refused to enter into an arranged marriage, are victims of trafficking, or have resisted or challenged social and cultural expectations. At least a dozen countries around the world now have provisions in their national asylum legislation opening up the possibility for people who have fled persecution because of their sexual orientation or gender identity to be recognized as refugees.

The key to many claims is the issue of whether there is a failure of the country of origin to protect the applicant from the harm that she faces. In other words asylum will be granted only if the applicant's home state cannot or will not protect her from the gender-related violence that she would face if she returned.[112] However, some women refugees have been denied asylum because the violence they suffered was committed by an armed group, not the state.

In international refugee law, there is a prohibition against returning someone to a territory where her life or freedom would be threatened because of who she is or what she believes. This is the principle of non-*refoulement*. In international human rights law there is a more general prohibition against *refoulement* where an individual would be at risk of serious human rights abuses, including torture. This general prohibition on *refoulement* is considered to be a norm of customary international law and therefore binding on all states.

Gender-related claims for protection can be linked to all five grounds for protection in the refugee definition (race, religion, nationality, political opinion and membership of a particular social group). An authoritative Conclusion adopted by the Executive Committee (EXCOM) of the UN High Commissioner for Refugees (UNHCR) states that "women asylum seekers who face harsh or inhuman treatment due to their having transgressed the social mores of the society in which they live may be considered as a 'particular social group'" facing persecution.

Refugees: a definition	The 1951 Convention relating to the Status of Refugees defines a refugee as any person who: "owing to well-founded fear of being persecuted for reasons of race, religion, nationality, membership of

a particular social group or political opinion, is outside the country of [her] nationality and is unable or, owing to such fear, is unwilling to avail [her]self of the protection of that country; or who, not having a nationality and being outside the country of [her] former habitual residence as a result of such events, is unable or, owing to such fear, is unwilling to return to it."

A woman making an asylum claim may not need to point to membership of a "particular social group" as the only ground on which she can claim protection from gender-related persecution. UNHCR has issued Guidelines on Gender-Related Persecution which recognize that:

"in many gender-related claims, the persecution feared could be for one, or more, of the Convention grounds. For example, a claim for refugee status based on transgression of social or religious norms may be analysed in terms of religion, political opinion or membership of a particular social group. The claimant is not required to identify accurately the reason why he or she has a well-founded fear of being persecuted."

Women sometimes have difficulty presenting their asylum claims because they may be ashamed or afraid to report the violations they have suffered. Where immigration officials lack specialist training this problem is compounded because they may not understand the difficulties women have when asked to recount their experiences of violence, harassment or discrimination.

Women's groups are using international law not only to persuade governments to accept their responsibilities, but also to gain protection for individual women. A Saudi Arabian woman who sought asylum in Canada because she had been harassed and threatened for not wearing a veil was initially denied refugee status because Canada did not recognize gender-based persecution as a ground for refugee status. Due to public pressure, the Canadian government announced it would allow her to stay, but only on humanitarian grounds. In 1993, amid public outcry over her case and several similar cases, Canada adopted new guidelines to recognize gender-based persecution as a ground for asylum.

The experience of violence that forces women and girls to become refugees may have a severe and long-lasting impact. In some cases, returning them to their own country would entail a "re-traumatization" and stigmatization, especially if they have survived rape and other forms of sexual violence. International refugee law recognizes that, even where a situation has changed, there may be compelling reasons arising out of previous persecution that mean that a refugee should not have to return to her country of origin. Women and girls may also be vulnerable as witnesses even where perpetrators are brought to justice.

As well as defining who is a refugee, the Refugee Convention also recognizes a range of rights to which refugees are entitled. These rights are in addition to the rights to which they are entitled as human beings under other international human rights instruments. Not least are the right to non-discrimination found in various human rights instruments, and rights enjoyed by women and girl refugees under the UN Convention on the Rights of the Child and CEDAW.

© AP

Demonstrators oppose violence against women at a protest in Port-au-Prince, Haiti, in front of the Palace of Justice.

Chapter 7. Impunity – violence unchecked and unpunished

Rita Margarete Rogerio, a Brazilian national, was arrested by Spanish police during a search for undocumented foreign sex workers in August 1995. No connection between her and sex work was ever established. She was raped in a cell in the main police station in Bilbao. Despite medical evidence, the public prosecutor refused to bring a case against the officer. When she brought a private prosecution, the court found that she had been beaten and raped, but felt obliged to acquit the three officers on duty at the time because they refused to testify against each other. In 1999 the Supreme Court described the acquittal for rape as "horrifying" because, while a lower court had found it "luminously clear" that Rita Rogerio had been raped by a uniformed officer in police custody, the police witnesses had conspired to lie, refusing to identify the rapist. As a result the Supreme Court had no alternative but to uphold the acquittal. Later, she faced a fierce press campaign against her by police officers and their union. After several rounds of trials, on 27 May 1999, two officers, who Rita Rogerio claimed had witnessed the rape, were suspended from duty. On 22 March 2000, they were acquitted for lack of evidence.

This case is only one of many in which women have lodged complaints of rape and other sexual abuse in police custody in Spain. Undocumented foreign women appear to be particularly targeted for abuse by the Spanish police. As in many countries, police procedures are deficient, lawyers and doctors are impeded from conducting confidential interviews, and judicial proceedings are often unduly protracted. As a result, the perpetrators are not brought to justice, the truth is not discovered and the victims do not receive redress.

When it comes to violence in the home, the issue of responsibility and accountability is complex because usually the family, the community and the state are all implicated. Women who seek to expose abuse are told that it is a private matter, and as a result, domestic violence is committed with impunity in countries all over the world. In Amnesty International's experience, such impunity is a major factor in prolonging the pattern of violence.

When women pursue legal action, they are often faced with a hostile and abusive criminal justice system. Deeply held attitudes that denigrate women, deny them equal rights and portray them as property are built into many penal and family codes, criminal investigation procedures and rules of evidence, and customary legal systems. For example, in many penal codes, rape is considered to be a "crime of honour", placing the woman's morality and her sexual behaviour before the court for analysis, and thereby treating her as the suspect. If a woman has had an active sexual life, she may in effect be held to have given her "consent".

Impunity is rife in conflict zones. For example, large numbers of women and girls have been raped and killed by Russian forces in the conflict in Chechnya. Investigations into allegations of human rights violations by Russian soldiers are rare. Investigations that do take place are usually inadequate and hardly ever result in prosecutions. Far from holding the perpetrators to account, the Russian authorities have reportedly redeployed units accused of human rights violations for further tours of service in Chechnya.

Many Chechens are deeply suspicious of the Russian authorities and have little faith that any complaint they bring will result in a prosecution. Women victims of rape are particularly unlikely to come forward and register a complaint given the stigma surrounding rape in their society. The Russian authorities have allowed a climate of impunity to emerge in Chechnya which protects and encourages human rights abusers.

© Paula Allen

The limitations of criminal justice solutions

The repeal or reform of discriminatory laws and practices has been a key focus of women's anti-violence advocacy. The five-year review of the Beijing Declaration and Platform for Action called for the repeal of discriminatory legislation by 2005. In response to growing activism, many countries have engaged in legal reform processes, as well as in training members of the criminal justice system.

Kheda Kungaeva's mother, Rosa, at the entrance to the tent where she lives. In March 2000, 18-year-old Kheda Kungaeva was seized from her home in Chechnya and taken to the tent of Russian army Colonel Yurii Budanov for interrogation. She was later found dead. She had been tortured and strangled and there was evidence suggesting that she had been raped. In July 2003, Yurii Budanov was found guilty of kidnapping, murder and exceeding the authority of his office, and sentenced to 10 years' imprisonment. The conviction was unprecedented – most violence in Chechnya is committed with complete impunity.

However, as women's groups and networks have gained experience, they have also recognized the challenges of this strategy. Even when the law prohibits violence against women, social institutions, cultural norms and political structures in every country sustain and maintain it, making the law a dead letter. Impunity remains the norm because of inadequate implementation, monitoring, documentation and evaluation of the law. Acts of violence against women therefore go unchecked and unpunished.

Discriminatory attitudes within the criminal justice system can undermine law reforms and lead to perverse outcomes, where women's rights, rather than being enhanced, are further restricted – women are under-policed but over-criminalized. In the USA, rape crisis centres have documented how victims are sometimes penalized because of poorly drafted or poorly implemented legislation.[113] Women from marginalized communities may be particularly reluctant to press charges or act as witnesses, having little or no confidence in the outcome of interaction with the police and criminal justice system.

Some progress has been made in holding to account perpetrators of violence against women at the international level. However, this is often not reflected in national prosecutions. For example, despite the ground-breaking decisions of the International Criminal Tribunal for the former Yugoslavia in prosecuting sexual violence, there have been no domestic prosecutions solely for rape in Bosnia-Herzegovina.

Bosnia-Herzegovina faces a vast legacy of unresolved human rights violations, including a large number of abuses against women and girls during the war, for which only a small number of perpetrators have been brought to justice. War crimes prosecutions before Bosnian courts have in general been flawed and many have collapsed after witnesses withdrew statements after intimidation and harassment. As the International Criminal Tribunal for the former Yugoslavia draws near its end, a Special Chamber of the State Court in Bosnia-Herzegovina has been proposed to prosecute war crimes. This new mechanism is weak on several counts, in particular the lack of attention given to the protection of women witnesses and their need for counselling and access to support.

During the conflict in Sierra Leone, rape and sexual violence were widespread and systematic. An amnesty was granted to all combatants under the 1999 Lomé peace agreement, which was subsequently passed into law, ruling out prosecutions for crimes committed during the conflict. The UN Security Council subsequently agreed that a Special Court for Sierra Leone should be established to try those bearing the greatest responsibility for crimes against humanity, war crimes and other serious violations of international humanitarian law. However, the Special Court can only look at crimes committed after 30 November 1996. The general amnesty is not a bar to prosecution by the Special Court, but it remains a serious impediment to gaining justice for the thousands of women and girls who suffered appalling abuses during the conflict.

Impunity encoded in law is the exception, although it features in a number of countries emerging from conflict. More common are laws that are inadequate, police forces that are uninterested, criminal justice systems that are remote, expensive and biased against women, and communities that still do not take violence against women seriously.

Flawed laws

There are flaws in the legal framework of some countries which contribute to impunity. For example, even though constitutional provisions may affirm women's right to a life free from violence, the definition may not cover all forms of violence against all women. Among the forms most frequently absent from legislative prohibition is sexual harassment in the workplace or in school. Laws may cover some forms of violence but not others – for example, the law may punish domestic violence, but may omit marital rape from the definition. This is the case in countries with otherwise progressive domestic violence legislation, such as Thailand.[114]

Laws against violence against women – especially domestic violence – frequently emphasize family reunification or maintenance over protecting victims. In some countries laws allow so-called "honour crimes" or allow a defence of honour to mitigate criminal penalties, putting the right of the family to defend its honour ahead of the rights of individuals in the family.

A woman waits at a centre for battered women in the Moroccan capital, Rabat. She has been beaten by her husband for more than 15 years and has nowhere else to go.

In some legal systems, the state will recognize a defence of honour, passion or provocation only on behalf of a husband in cases of alleged adultery. In others, sons, fathers, uncles and so on may also be immune from punishment for engaging in violence and ill-treatment. In those cases where the state has crafted formal legal exemptions or reduced sentences for family-member homicides invoking honour, it fails a strict test of the state's responsibility to respect rights. In other cases, the failure to investigate or prosecute contravenes the state's responsibility to protect rights and exercise due diligence. This lack of due diligence on the part of the state can have fatal consequences. In Lebanon, according to the Penal Code, a man who kills his wife or other female relative may receive a reduced sentence if he demonstrates that he committed the crime in response to a socially unacceptable sexual relationship conducted by the victim. There were an average of two to three such crimes committed each month in Lebanon in 2001, but by February 2003 no one had yet been convicted in a case legally considered to be an "honour crime".[115]

Some countries, such as Brazil, Lebanon and Turkey, have laws that suspend rape sentences if the perpetrator marries the victim. Reporting on penal code reform in Argentina that substituted "Crimes Against Sexual Integrity" for the previously named "Crimes Against Decency", the Center for Reproductive Rights observes:

"With regard to rape, the possibility for rapists to enter into an agreement has replaced the previous provision that allowed rapists to escape punishment by marrying the victim. Despite the change, this rule continues to allow the rapist to avoid criminal liability by replacing the notion of a crime having occurred with the notion of a conflict that can be negotiated."[116]

Sometimes the detailed provisions of a law undermine its stated purpose. In Egypt, for example, there is a law prohibiting female genital mutilation, but it refers only to operations performed outside hospitals by people without a medical qualification.[117]

Discriminatory laws

In some countries, even if legislation does not condone violence directly, it is discriminatory – the laws treat women differently from men, and confer fewer or lesser rights on women. Examples of such gender bias in statutory law include women being unable to sign official documents without their husband's permission or needing their husband's consent in order to get a passport, use contraception, or acquire property. Women in many countries have fewer rights than men to inheritance or property ownership. In many countries, including Gabon, a wife must get her husband's permission to travel abroad.[118] In other countries, women are unable to pass their citizenship on to their children. Many women are thus trapped in abusive situations, or face the invidious choice of staying or leaving without their children.

A 16-year-old Afghan girl who had "run away" from her 85-year-old husband whom she had been forced to marry at the age of nine was sentenced to two and a half years' imprisonment for *zina*. The man who helped her escape was reportedly released after five months.

Sometimes there is gender bias in the application of the law. Under Afghan law, adultery is a criminal offence carrying a prison sentence of up to 10 years or, where certain evidentiary requirements are met, the punishment of stoning. (To Amnesty International's knowledge, this punishment has not been applied during the transitional period.) In many parts of Afghanistan, there is a strong emphasis on prosecuting girls and women for offences such as adultery, "running away from home" and sex before marriage, which are known as *zina* crimes. A few men have been accused or convicted of *zina* crimes, but the criminal justice system places disproportionate emphasis on the prosecution of women for *zina* crimes.

Failure to implement the law

Even where the legal framework outlawing violence against women is in place, it may fail at the implementation stage. For example, the appropriate enabling legislation may not be passed, or inadequate provisions might be made for enforcement. Jurisdiction may not be unambiguously established, and if and when it is, judges may prefer to use civil, rather than criminal, codes resulting in much more lenient treatment of acts of violence.

In some areas, there appears to be no attempt to implement the law. For example, early marriages of girls are common in many countries despite legislative prohibitions against them, and international obligations set out in the UN Convention on the Rights of the Child, defining the age of 18 as the outer boundary of childhood. Article 24(3) obliges states to take all effective and appropriate measures with a view to abolishing traditional practices prejudicial to the health of children, and the Committee on the Rights of the Child has determined that child and forced marriage is both a harmful traditional practice and a form of gender discrimination. The UN-NGO Working Group on Girls reports that the youngest brides are likely to have husbands many years their senior. Indeed, they report that "the younger the bride, the greater the age difference with the spouse; 35 per cent of the partners of married adolescent girls aged 15-19 in the less developed countries (excluding China) are 10 or more years older."[119]

In Kosovo, a law prohibiting trafficking of women was promulgated in February 2001, but by July 2003, provisions to protect victims and provide compensation had not yet been implemented by the UN Mission in Kosovo, which governs the former Serbian province.[120] Women continued to be arrested and prosecuted for offences including prostitution and passport or border violations. Members of the international peace-keeping and civilian police forces suspected of involvement in trafficking or the use of the services of trafficked women or girls have not faced prosecution, despite relevant provisions in the law.[121]

Women from Kyrgyzstan in mourning for their husbands and brothers, allegedly shot by police in the village of Kerben in March 2002. In 2003 they travelled to the capital Bishkek and went on hunger-strike to demand that those responsible were brought to trial.

© Vyacheslav Oseledko

Those who administer the criminal justice system – judges, prosecutors, police, prison guards – are not immune from the pervasive view that women are responsible for violence committed against them or that they deserve to be punished for non-conforming behaviour. This is reflected in the administration of justice – in most countries the law is applied in a discriminatory manner. As a result, cases of violence against women often founder unless there is clear and unavoidable evidence of force, illustrating to all that the victim "fought back". In court proceedings the testimony of female victims is frequently undermined by irrelevant evidence of previous sexual history and aggressive cross-examination by lawyers. Sometimes women complainants have been cross-examined by the accused person representing himself. Sometimes evidence of psychiatric assistance – whether linked to the rape or not – has been used to portray her as unreliable. Research conducted in Vancouver, Canada, for the period from 1993 to 1997 found that the biggest predictor of convictions in rape cases was the presence of physical injuries on the victim. In addition, the study showed that convictions are rare: in the group of 462 cases reviewed, only 33 per cent resulted in charges being laid, and only 11 per cent in convictions.[122]

In some cases, the rules of evidence are impossible to meet because there are few forensic doctors available to perform the appropriate examinations, or because the victim may be required to pay for the forensic examination and cannot afford to do so. In St. Cloud, Minnesota, USA, for example, rape victims may be required to pay for a hospital's collection of evidence from the assault. This is increasingly the case in states across the USA and in many countries throughout the world.[123]

In some cases, especially in conflicts, women are unable to reach a doctor quickly. The process of providing evidence can be harrowing. Even when examinations are conducted and the case goes to trial, the manner of the proceedings may deter women from persisting with charges.

A Kenyan woman who alleged she had been raped described the ordeal of providing evidence:

"After I had been taken to a private doctor, he told me not to wash as I would have to report to the police doctor. Since it was 2am, this meant that my report would have to be filed on the next day. I could not believe that I would have to sleep with the smell of those men on me... When I went to report to the police doctor, I found a long line with all sorts of people. The nurse assisting him gave me two glass slides and told me to stick my fingers up myself and wipe the semen onto the glass slide. I could not believe what she was saying to me, they were asking me to re-enact the rape."[124]

For women from marginalized communities, indifference and hostility from the police is common – especially if the perpetrator is from the majority community.

In India, *dalits*[125] face daily abuse and violence. In one case in Uttar Pradesh, Ramvathi was gang-raped by five men in September 1998. It is believed that higher caste villagers raped her in order to punish her and her husband Ram Chandra for refusing to give up a piece of land and to isolate them from the *dalit* community through the stigma attached to rape. When Ram Chandra went to lodge a complaint with the police, they refused to file a report. Finally, the Superintendent of Police in the district ordered the incident to be investigated, but no action was taken. Some months later, when the couple tried to reclaim their property, they were severely beaten by men armed with sticks and axes. Ramvathi was raped with a stick and died the next day. After activists put pressure on the Superintendent of Police, a report was filed, but as of March 2003, no evidence had been placed before the court. Such failure by the state to investigate and prosecute cases of violence against women is a signal of a failure of due diligence.

Agnes Siyiankoi, the first Maasai woman to take her husband to court for beating her. In October 1998 a Kenyan magistrate found her husband guilty as charged and sentenced him to six months' imprisonment and a fine. For having the courage to speak out, Agnes Siyiankoi was severely criticized and labelled a traitor to Maasai culture.

In far too many cases, the state works hand in hand with private actors to justify, condone or excuse violence against women committed by families, business enterprises and other private actors. Such is the case in Indonesia, where Indonesians wishing to work abroad as domestics have to go through private recruitment agencies. These agencies often send prospective workers to training camps for long periods – lasting several months to a year. There are hundreds of these camps across the country, and although minimal standards have been set by the government they are rarely enforced. The non-governmental organization Anti-Slavery International documented the story of Adek, who hoped for work in Hong Kong. Through a broker, Adek was connected with an employment agency in Surabaya, East Java, where she paid for a medical test, uniform and books. Adek was sent to a training camp in Surabaya, along with about 1,000 other women. Conditions were bad, food was scarce, the water was dirty and many women fell ill. While Adek was there, one woman died because of lack of medical care. The women were forced to work for the agency staff, were not allowed to leave and were permitted only short and infrequent family visits. Adek's letters were censored and she was forced to sign contract papers without understanding them. After four months, she was taken to Hong Kong, but was not paid anything for her work at the camp.[126]

The failure to respect women's rights is shown whenever agents of the state are themselves the perpetrators of violence. Community United Against Violence, in San Francisco, USA, has observed that law enforcement officers frequently assume that all transsexual women are sex workers, and arrest and charge them with prostitution even when they are alone, with their husbands or partners.[127] According to one account:

"Stephanie was walking to a night club when she noticed a police car following…When she arrived at the bar, she immediately went into the women's bathroom…a police officer barged into the bathroom, grabbed her and arrested her for prostitution. Later at the precinct, he started to strip-search her with everyone taunting her. One officer pulled her hair so hard, claiming it was a wig, that her scalp began to bleed. She was thrown into a cell naked and left in the cold night. She had no criminal record but was charged with solicitation."[128]

Some governments avoid their responsibilities towards women's human rights by claiming that, as a state in transition, the legislative framework necessary is not yet in place. In countries with a federal structure, state and federal authorities have on occasion each claimed that the other bore responsibility. For example, in Mexico, for many years the federal authorities refused to take responsibility for investigations into the abductions and killings in Ciudad Juárez on the grounds that these were state, rather than federal, crimes.

Community complicity

At the local level, when the suffering of women victims of violence is ignored or disparaged, impunity is reinforced. The following story is typical of many. On 12 February 2001 a young Burmese lesbian working in Thailand and a male friend were returning home when several men who worked at the same factory joined them. They were drunk. One of them asked her if she was a lesbian. She said nothing, but started to walk faster. They blocked her way, one of them told her that she was beautiful, and said that it was a waste for her to be a lesbian. He grabbed her and told his friends to "cure this abnormal lesbian so she can enter womanhood." All six men raped her, and left when they were finished. The next day, the whole factory knew about the rape, but no one came to her defence. In tears, she asked why the community allowed these rapists to go unpunished and blamed only her. As a female migrant worker, this woman was particularly vulnerable to abuse. Female migrant workers in Thailand have also been raped by Thai security forces; a young Karen woman from Myanmar (Burma) was raped by a Thai policeman who had promised to take her safely to Bangkok for employment. Neither she nor the Burmese lesbian dared report the rapes to the Thai authorities for fear of being arrested and deported.

When women depart from what the community holds to be "appropriate" behaviour, whether by asserting their sexuality or in other ways, they are often met with violent retribution – by their families, members of the community, or the state. Common forms include abductions, rapes, killings and incarceration. In many societies, marriage patterns and customs already infringe upon the fundamental rights of women and men to equally choose their spouse, to consent to sexual activity in marriage or to end a marriage. So women may transgress community norms merely by seeking to assert their fundamental rights. This structural violence puts women's rights to life and bodily integrity at risk. The state remains accountable for ensuring women's basic rights, even when they choose to depart from community norms. In the struggle against impunity, the silent complicity of not only the state, but also individuals and communities, has to be confronted and overcome.

In Switzerland, a Cameroonian women residing legally in the country was detained on a Geneva street with her five-week-old baby after a dispute over a bus fare. She alleges that the police handcuffed her, subjected her to physical and racial abuse, strip-searched her in front of male officers and separated her from her unweaned baby. Only after the intervention of a doctor in the police station was the baby returned to her. Another doctor examined her after her release and found signs of injury and shock. Her complaint was dismissed by the cantonal judicial authorities although she was never questioned and no attempt was made to obtain statements from witnesses such as the two doctors who examined her.

Amina Lawal (*right*) was sentenced to be stoned to death for *zina* (sexual relations outside marriage) by a Shari'a court in Nigeria. The Shari'a legal system co-exists with the federal legal system in Nigeria. The man she named as the father of her baby reportedly denied having sex with her and the charges against him were discontinued. After an international campaign and a legal defence mounted by a coalition of women's groups, the conviction was overturned on appeal.

Chapter 8. Parallel legal systems

In a range of countries and communities, traditional authorities or customary law operate alongside the formal, statutory legal system. Village elders, religious courts, traditional chiefs or clan structures operate quasi-formal legal systems in parallel to statutory law, sometimes informally but with social legitimacy, sometimes with powers formally granted to them by the state. These parallel legal regimes monitor and control community norms and practices, which often means reinforcing male power over women and permitting violence against women. Amnesty International believes that parallel justice systems are not an adequate replacement for an effective criminal justice system that respects and ensures the rights of victims to full reparations and the accused's right to a fair trial.

Sometimes the parallel system is built into the structure of the formal legal system. In Israel, for example, civil marriage and divorce do not exist. For Israeli Jews, all such unions are governed by the Rabbinic court. In order for a woman to get a divorce, she needs either the consent of her husband or the Rabbinic court to take action on her behalf. Often the Rabbinic courts suggest that couples work it out themselves, "even when they know divorce is unavoidable… [indirectly] forcing women to give in to their husband's financial blackmail".[129] Jewish women denied divorces are described as *agunot* (literally "chained women"), neither married nor divorced and unable to remarry or pursue their lives.

Sometimes parallel legal regimes only encompass particular communities. In several states in northern Nigeria, new legislation which is based on concepts of Islamic Shari'a law has been introduced in addition to previously enacted Nigerian statutory law. These laws are only valid for people of Muslim faith. They prescribe the death sentence for offences such as sexual intercourse outside marriage which were previously not punishable by death but by lashing, which is in itself a cruel, inhuman and degrading punishment. When the accused is not Muslim, similar offences are not considered criminal offences and are therefore not punishable.

In some countries, personal status law, family and customary law covering inheritance, property rights, marriage, divorce and custody deny women the same rights as men. These laws were frequently codified by the colonial powers. The legal codes tended to be very conservative interpretations of religious or customary law. In Kenya customary laws are mostly unwritten, but the country's legal system formally recognizes them. However, Human Rights Watch has documented how customary law is fluid and subjective. One senior chief told Human Rights Watch interviewers, "Customary law is what I describe."[130]

In a widely reported case from Pakistan, Mukhtaran Bibi, a 30-year-old woman of the Gujjar tribe in Meerwala, Punjab province, was sentenced in June 2002 by a "tribal court" to being gang-raped. The sentence was as punishment for her younger brother's alleged "illicit affair" with a girl from another tribe, the Mastoi, considered higher in the tribal hierarchy. Several hundred villagers stood by while the sentence was carried out. Only after a local cleric mentioned the case and a journalist picked it up did local police take action. It later came to light that the entire "illicit affair" was concocted to cover up the sexual abuse of Mukhtaran Bibi's brother by three men of the Mastoi tribe.

In some countries the state itself creates or generates the parallel system. In Rwanda, for example, the professionally trained national police force constitutes only a small percentage of the country's internal security mechanism. In the hillsides of Rwanda, young men with virtually no training in policing methods or human rights are given uniforms and guns and sent to patrol the communities. No law has yet been passed to regulate the operations of these "Local Defence Forces" (LDF). Members of the LDF have been accused of sexual violence and assault on women in the communities for which they are supposed to be providing security. When accused, members of the LDF are rarely tried, and in the few trials that have been held, the accused have been released in a matter of days, according to the information received by Amnesty International. One member of the LDF who was charged with rape was taken to court and released two days later, at which point he allegedly raped another woman. This process was repeated five times and he was identified by all five women as the rapist. There are also allegations that LDF members have forced women into marriage.

In other communities, parallel authorities operate outside the law but with near-complete power within their area of influence. In Jamaica, well-defined poor, urban communities or neighbourhoods known as garrisons are controlled by gangs, headed by a don. According to one report, in garrisons "disputes have been settled, matters tried, offenders sentenced and punished, all without reference to the institutions of the Jamaican State."[131] Forced sex may be the payment required for gang protection of poor women. One Jamaican women's rights activist explains, "In most inner-city communities, as soon as a girl reaches puberty, she is sent for by any man who wants to have sex with her, starting with the don... gang-rapes were used to show women who resisted men's sexual advances 'that they did not have authority over their own bodies'."[132] These same informal authorities may also take action against rapes reported to them. In the informal system of garrison justice, some men may even be killed for it.[133]

In Bangladesh, local religious leaders have issued *fatwas*, or religious edicts, which often call for flogging, stoning and other humiliating punishments, such

as shaving of heads, insults and beatings. Recently, *fatwas* have been issued by rural religious leaders at village gatherings against women who assert themselves in village life. A landmark High Court ruling on 1 January 2001, delivered by two renowned judges including Nazmun Ara Sultana, the first woman judge in the country, declared *fatwas* to be illegal. The ruling was welcomed by a cross section of civil society groups who urged the government to implement it immediately, but triggered strong opposition from a number of Islamist groups. There were violent demonstrations against the ruling, in which at least one police officer and seven Muslim activists were reportedly killed. The High Court ruling was put on hold by the Supreme Court on 14 January 2001, pending the hearing of a petition by two local religious leaders challenging it. As of July 2003, this petition had yet to be heard.

Survivors of the 1994 genocide in Rwanda listen to an official from the Ministry of Justice explaining how the newly revived *gacaca* courts (traditional community-based courts) will try people accused of participating in the genocide. The government of Rwanda has moved the cases of about 115,000 defendants accused of atrocities during the 1994 genocide into these courts in response to gross overcrowding in Rwandese prisons. During the election of judges for the *gacaca* courts, some judges were rejected because they were known to physically abuse their wives.

In militarized zones, another form of parallel authority takes hold – that of armed groups, including paramilitaries allied with the government. In

Colombia, for example, survivors of domestic violence reportedly do not turn to the family court or to the Attorney General's office,

"because they say that these institutions will not give them immediate service… Now they go and make requests of the paramilitaries [allied with the security forces] or the guerrillas since they say that they are more effective. 'I go to the commander of the paramilitaries, tell them my case, and immediately they come, take him, give him a beating and the second time he knows what's what, and that is all it takes.'"[134]

"Everyone shall have the right to be tried by ordinary courts or tribunals using established legal procedures. Tribunals that do not use the duly established procedures of the legal process shall not be created to displace the jurisdiction belonging to the ordinary courts or judicial tribunals."
UN Basic Principles on the Independence of the Judiciary, Principle 5.[135]

There is some evidence that parallel structures have gained power in recent years. As a result of corruption, inadequate resources and political tensions, some communities have reconstituted their own traditional justice systems to stand in for formal legal mechanisms. Amnesty International has documented how tribal councils in Pakistan have been convened to resolve disputes over land, water, breaches of "honour" and murder. Their objective is not to elicit the truth – which in a close-knit community is frequently widely known – but the restoration of social harmony. Tribal councils do this by imposing compensation payments on the offender. Compensation can be of different kinds; in land and water disputes it will be in the form of money. In case of "honour" crimes and murder, it can either be in monetary form or a woman or girl is given in compensation to the aggrieved party.[136]

State authorities have repeatedly shown themselves to be indifferent to the pervasive and growing power of tribal councils and other forms of parallel authority and they have often refused to hold the leaders accountable in the face of violations.

'Restorative' justice

While parallel legal regimes are most commonly thought of as contributing to discrimination against women, in some communities traditional methods of "restorative" justice are being pursued to address some of the deficiencies of the formal justice system. Restorative justice is a process which brings victims and offenders into contact and provides an opportunity for victims, offenders and sometimes representatives of the community to discuss an offence and how to repair the harm caused.

Women's organizations have taken the lead in building new models of conflict resolution based on cultural traditions. In India, *Mahila Panchayats* are women's collectives grounded in traditional community organization which seek to resolve disputes while preventing the need for legal intervention. They provide a space for aggrieved parties to speak openly and negotiate settlements, including in cases of domestic violence. Paralegal workers and legal counsel assist in the dispute resolution process. They build on long-standing community traditions, but reframe these cultural institutions to serve the needs of victims of violence and abuse.[137]

In the Indian state of West Bengal, the Shramajibee Mahila Samity (SMS), a non-affiliated mass organization of working women, holds 70-80 *salishis* each month. The *salishis* are a village level dispute resolution process. The SMS conducts them in order to deliver justice to survivors of domestic violence, on the understanding that many women simply want the violence to end, but do not want the marriage dissolved. The *salishis* give these women the opportunity to speak publicly without shame, and to negotiate a solution. In the formal legal system, they would expect little or nothing.[138]

Indigenous communities in Canada have experimented with community-based justice programs, which seek to bring all parties together to construct a healing contract. Everyone is assigned an advocate, and everyone is responsible for holding the perpetrator accountable to the contract.

Although restorative justice systems can play an important role in providing an informal space for victims to describe their experiences, they cannot be a substitute for a fair and effective criminal justice process. Restorative justice systems should respect due process, establish the truth, facilitate reparations to victims and make recommendations designed to prevent a repetition of crimes. They may complement the criminal justice system, but they cannot replace it.

There is a danger that alternative or restorative justice processes weaken an already weak formal criminal justice system. Furthermore, achieving results that are beneficial to women requires a community united in holding the perpetrator accountable. Sometimes, victims of violence are pressured into accepting agreements without sufficient support or concern for their security. Amnesty International believes that all perpetrators of crimes involving violations of human rights should be brought to justice.

Men and women at Amnesty International's International Council Meeting raise their hands in support of the Stop Violence against Women campaign. Mexico, August 2003.

© AI

Chapter 9. Organizing for change – making a difference

Violence against women is universal but it is not inevitable. A recent World Health Organization report points out that communities that condemn violence, take action to end it and provide support for survivors, have lower levels of violence than communities that do not take such action. In a comparative study of 16 countries, researchers found that levels of partner violence are lowest in those societies with community sanctions (whether in the form of legal action, social approbation or moral pressure) and sanctuaries (shelters or family support systems).[139]

All over the world women's rights activists have led efforts to expose violence against women; to give victims a voice; to provide innovative forms of support; to force governments and the international community to recognize their own failure to protect women; and to hold all those responsible to account. They have shown that organizing to combat violence against women can make a real difference. Amnesty International is launching a campaign to mobilize its more than 1.5 million members and supporters worldwide to add their voices to this struggle to stop violence against women.

Making rights matter

One of the main reasons for engaging a human rights framework to oppose violence against women is the credibility it lends to the claim that contesting violence against women is a public responsibility, requiring legal and social redress. It also makes the more powerful appeal that violence against women, no matter what the cultural context, is not a legitimate practice and that the individual woman's body is inviolable. Often, making this point has required courageous work on the part of women's organizations.

Increasingly this advocacy is backed up by research into violence against women. For example, since 1994, the Women's Centre for Legal Aid and

Counselling in Jerusalem (WCLAC) has worked with other women's groups to ensure that laws codifying "honour killings" have no place on the statute book if a Palestinian state is established.[140] Faced with a dearth of reliable information, since police and court records tend to accept the explanation of death by suicide or accident, WCLAC has been searching out accurate information. They have brought "honour killings" – which they have renamed *femicide* – into public view and have sought to broaden the definition from an act of murder to a method used to control women's sexuality and to punish women for non-compliance with social norms.[141] WCLAC has analyzed information from a variety of sources, including official records, clients, families of victims, health officials, police, and judges, and has conducted surveys and interviews.

Like all Palestinian women's organizations, WCLAC activists have had to overcome enormous obstacles. First, they must confront discrimination and violence against women in their own communities. Second, they work in a context of extreme hardship, insecurity and deprivation. Since the uprising (*intifada*) in September 2000, much of the work of Palestinian women's groups has had to switch its focus to deal with the violence of the occupation and conflict. Though most of the dead and prisoners are men, the impact on women is enormous. Three thousand homes and vast areas of cultivated land have been demolished. More than 2,000 people have been killed. Thousands of Palestinians have been imprisoned. Closures and curfews choke the movement of every Palestinian and impede their access to work, education, health care and contacts with family and friends. The destruction of the Palestinian economy has resulted in more than 60 per cent of Palestinians living below the poverty line. The responsibility for managing daily life in the face of privation – collecting and preparing food, water and fuel – falls disproportionately on women.

Naming violations

The suffering caused by acts of violence against women can be lifelong, and so can the struggle for redress. An estimated 200,000 women from across Asia were forced into military brothels during the Second World War by the Japanese Imperial Army. These so-called "comfort women" began demanding acknowledgement of the violations they had suffered only in the late 1980s and 1990s. By this time, some no longer had any family who might be "shamed" and women's activists had begun to link the issue with the problem of sexual oppression of women as a whole.[142]

In 1991, in response to a letter from the Korean Women's Association demanding an apology, a memorial and a thorough inquiry, the Japanese government claimed that there was no evidence of the forced drafting of Korean women as "comfort women", and thus no need for such action by the government of Japan. Anger at that response prompted many women to come forward and, in some cases, to file suits. In August 1991, a South Korean woman named Kim Hak-soon became the first former "comfort woman" to give public testimony.

Japan was reluctant to even acknowledge the existence of "comfort women", doing so only in 1992, and references to their plight appeared for the first time in Japanese school textbooks in 1994. A private fund, rather than an official fund, was set up to pay compensation.

In 1998 a Japanese district court ruled in favour of three South Korean women who had filed a suit against Japan. However, the Hiroshima High Court over-ruled the decision, in line with the Japanese government's argument that it need not pay compensation to the women as all claims were settled by peace treaties that formally ended the war. None of the other cases filed have succeeded.

The Masisukumeni women's crisis centre, Tonga, South Africa. The centre was established in 1994 in a poor rural area to support and assist survivors of violence against women, to uphold their human and legal rights, and to work against gender violence through education programs.

Although individual representatives of the Japanese government have issued a series of apologies, they have not spoken for the government as a whole. Japan has made no acknowledgment of legal liability and has undertaken no prosecutions.

In 2001, the non-governmental Women's International War Crimes Tribunal concluded that Japan's late Emperor Hirohito, and his government, were responsible for forcing women into sexual slavery during the Second World War. It described the system as "state-sanctioned rape and enslavement".

Break the silence . . .

© UNIFEM

. . .say no to violence against women and girls

Raising awareness

Anti-violence activists – from grass-roots, community-based initiatives, to large national and regional networks, to international organizations and UN agencies – have engaged in a wide variety of efforts to break the silence about violence against women, educate women about their rights, teach men that violence against women is a human rights abuse and a crime, and mobilize communities to take responsibility for ending violence against women.

In Senegal, a non-governmental organization, Tostan ("breakthrough" in Wolof), designed a village-level human rights education program, with a strong emphasis on participatory learning. Entire villages – men, women, religious leaders and traditional chiefs – were involved. They started by teaching villagers about their human rights, including those in CEDAW, followed by sessions including problem-solving and reproductive health in which participants identified their needs. During this process communities themselves invariably identified female genital mutilation as a problem and engaged in debate about ending the practice. After the first phase, in November 1999, around 80,000 people from 105 villages throughout the Kolda region participated in a ceremony at which they issued a public declaration to end the practice of female genital mutilation.[143]

In 1998 and 1999, several regional offices of the United Nations Development Fund for Women (UNIFEM) spearheaded high-profile regional campaigns to end violence against women. These campaigns – held first in Latin America and the Caribbean, then in Asia and the Pacific, followed by Africa, and most recently in central and eastern Europe and central Asia – have received a great deal of public attention and, in some cases, have brought about changes in law and policy. Involving UN agencies, governments and non-governmental organizations, and using the media, these campaigns have promoted the message that all people, not only women, are responsible for ending violence against women.

Larger and larger networks have been formed globally and in all regions of the world. For example, women's groups in the Southern Cone of Latin America formed the Southern Cone Network Against Domestic Violence in 1989; in 1990, representatives from 21 countries formed the Latin American and Caribbean Network Against Domestic and Sexual Violence. The campaigns conducted by these organizations and networks have resulted in significant

In 1981, the first Latin American and Caribbean Feminist Encuentro (Meeting) declared 25 November an International Day for No Violence Against Women, to commemorate the killing of the Mirabal sisters by members of the security forces of the Trujillo government in the Dominican Republic in 1960. In 1987, Puerto Rico officially recognized the day. In 1999, the UN declared 25 November to be the International Day for the Elimination of Violence against Women.

changes in national legislative and policy environments, as well as regional and international statements of political will. For instance, almost all countries in Latin America and the Caribbean have legislation on domestic or family violence. Many have laws that address sexual violence, including both amendments to the penal codes and the inclusion of provisions that specifically address sexual violence.[144]

Engaging human rights mechanisms

Non-governmental organizations and legal advocates have used international human rights law not only to raise awareness and build pressure on governments but also more directly. In some cases, the injunction to abide by international human standards has taken hold in courts and criminal proceedings. The Turkish Constitutional Court has extensively referred to CEDAW in decisions whose effect, among other things, has been to decriminalize adultery.[145] Only two weeks after its ratification by Afghanistan, Amnesty International observed the Chief Judge of the District Court of Kabul considering CEDAW in a case in which a husband who had left for several years returned to find that his wife had married again. The husband was asking the court to force her to return to him and to have her prosecuted for adultery. At the same time, she was petitioning for a divorce, due to desertion, at the advice of the National Human Rights Commission. In a lower court, the judge had refused to deal with the case, noting the country's recent ratification of CEDAW, and arguing that the judgment he would have normally delivered would conflict with women's rights to equality. The Chief Judge, noting the conflict of rights, decided to refer the case to the Chief Justice of the Supreme Court.

Regional human rights systems have also been an important site for combating discriminatory laws and demanding an end to impunity. Women's activists have harnessed regional human rights systems in order to hold their governments accountable and receive reparations. For example, the Latin American Commission for the Defense of Women's Rights (Comité Latino Americano de

© UNIFEM, UNDP & FIDA

**'HE WANTS A BABY BOY'
GENDER VIOLENCE
BEGINS HERE.**

It begins with the unborn child.

Long before it's been named or drawn its first breath. Once born, the child's worth again will be measured according to its sex. And if it is a girl, the first words she hears her father say to her mother may well be 'What kind of a woman are you? I wanted a boy!'

In time, that child will grow into a woman. She will marry and, like her mother, seek to fulfil her life's worth by bearing a son.

It's time to break the cycle. To recognize that all human beings are born equal. To raise all our children to be all they can be. The resposibility rests with us.

VIOLENCE AGAINST WOMEN. NOBODY WINS

This message is sponsored by United Nations Development Fund for Women (UNIFEM), United Nations Development Program (UNDP) in collaboration with Federation of Women Lawyers (FIDA)

Defensa de los Derechos de la Mujer, CLADEM) has filed claims before the Inter-American Commission on Human Rights, drawing on the Inter-American Convention on the Prevention, Punishment and Eradication of Violence against Women, and the American Convention on Human Rights. At the time of writing, for example, procedures had been initiated in a case pertaining to sexual violence, and in a case on forced sterilization.[146]

Harnessing community responsibility

Accountability is not only a question for the state – violence against women is also sustained by lack of accountability at the individual and community level. At the community level, some of the "solutions" have themselves created new challenges. In Cambodia, the Cambodia Women's Crisis Center (CWCC) has created a system of community coalitions – involving the police, community leaders and trained activist/monitors to intervene in situations of domestic violence. The coalition develops a contract between the batterer and the victim, and together they monitor the batterer's adherence to the contract. In this way, CWCC argues, the issue of domestic violence has been transformed from a private issue suffered by women in silence, to a public issue understood as requiring community participation and change. However, many of the communities in which CWCC has conducted training have seen an increase in domestic disputes. It appeared that some men were uncomfortable with the idea of their wives' participation. Some objected to their wives being absent from serving meals. In response, CWCC went from house to house to encourage men to attend the sessions and to allow their wives to do so as well. Many men still refused to participate, but CWCC has continued to work in the communities with volunteers and the police to develop community-based solutions.[147]

Civil sanctions

Women's rights activists in some countries are promoting various forms of civil sanctions as well as criminal penalties as a means of countering and redressing violence against women. Such civil sanctions can include protection orders, fines, and removal from the home. For example, in Italy, judges can order payments to victims who lack resources, including through withholding the sum from the aggressor's pay.[148] In Colombia and Costa Rica, aggressors may be required to attend public or private centres for therapy.[149]

In Colombia, El Salvador, Guatemala and Paraguay, measures to protect victims of violence include temporary restraining orders banning the perpetrators from the household. Such protection orders, often a function of municipal rather than national government, also exist in Barbados, Turkey, the USA, and many western European countries. However, women often find that protection orders are not vigorously applied. In a case reported by Women's Aid in Dublin, Ireland, a survivor of repeated attacks by her husband had received a three-year barring order to keep her husband away from her. Despite this, he continued to harass her, coming to her house and threatening to kill her and her friends, smashing her car and phoning her house all night long. Following one of these incidents he was arrested and sentenced to one year's probation. After another incident, he was again arrested and given a custodial sentence, which he appealed. He was released on bail, and allowed to see his children. At a judicial separation hearing several months later, the court refused to hear evidence about his abuse, saying that it had no bearing on the case. As a result, he was awarded joint custody of the children.

Family: a definition	The term family has often been understood as meaning the nuclear family, but there are many different forms of family, such as extended families, single parent families and families with parents of the same sex. An inclusive approach would treat the family as the site of intimate personal relationships, rather than as an institution defined by the state.

A law enacted in Germany in 2001 allows courts to order perpetrators out of the home so that victims are not forced to seek refuge in shelters. One of the innovations of this law is that it applies not only to legally married couples but also to couples who live together but are not married.

Demanding local action

Advocates for ending violence against women have also sought to harness the capacity of local, regional and municipal government. Human rights organizations have traditionally focused on holding states accountable at the national level for their failure to protect rights and ensure access to justice and adequate protection for women escaping violence. In many countries, however, local and municipal governments control education, rights in marriage and access to key services for women. They are also often responsible for protection through the police, courts, shelters and hospitals. In light of this, anti-violence activists are "bringing human rights home," engaging in advocacy at the local level to make governments more accountable and to challenge unbridled impunity.

Sometimes, the injunction to "bring human rights home" has been taken literally. In San Francisco, USA, women's groups mobilized to pass a local ordinance incorporating the main components of CEDAW into municipal law. One of its main elements is a gender-sensitive review of the city's budgeting process, to ensure gender equity in the distribution of resources. A similar initiative incorporating CEDAW into local law was passed in Buenos Aires, Argentina, among other municipalities around the world.

In Brazil, special women's police stations and desks have been set up, and, increasingly, women are allowed to give their statements in privacy. The idea is to have staff specifically trained to deal with violence against women. However many believe that these women's police stations have not lived up to their promise. Often the police officers who staff them are very low-level officers, who sometimes feel that they are sent to these stations as punishment.

These efforts at police reform, while important, touch only the edges of the deep changes required in local government. What is needed is a justice system that looks to prevent violence against women, provide appropriate services, support and remedies, and to hold the perpetrators accountable in ways that provide lasting results.

Women have taken enormous strides to counter violence and achieve justice and equality. They have organized support services – sometimes with, though often without, the support of their governments; they have initiated local, national and international campaigns to raise awareness about the rampant nature of violence against women and to shame their governments into taking action; they have lobbied for the repeal of discriminatory laws and the adoption of legislation to address violence against women; they have developed national, regional and international networks that have changed the face of global organizing; and one by one, they have confronted their abusers, left violent situations, and claimed their right to live free from violence. In the face of the pervasive shame and stigma attached to women speaking out about violence committed against them, they have asserted – "silent no more".

© The Irish Times

Amnesty International's Agenda for Change

Fifty-five pairs of shoes laid out in Dublin Castle represent women murdered in Ireland by men known to them. This exhibit marked the 25th anniversary of Women's Aid in Ireland in 2000.

In the home and in the community, in times of war and peace, women and girls are beaten, raped, mutilated and killed with impunity. Violence and the threat of violence affect the ability of all women to exercise their civil, political, social, economic and cultural rights and diminish all our lives. As long as violence against women continues, the promise to humanity of the Universal Declaration of Human Rights cannot be fulfilled.

This is not to deny the achievements of the women's and human rights movements at international, national and local levels, but to acknowledge that countless women face physical, sexual and mental abuse at the hands of close relatives as well as strangers. All too often, communities tolerate violence against women and deny women the freedom to choose how to live their lives. Local, regional and national authorities fail to prevent and punish acts of violence, and do not provide an environment free from violence. In conflict zones, both government forces and armed groups commit atrocities against women with impunity. Internationally, the performance of UN bodies is uneven and in many areas should be significantly improved, while international financial institutions and corporations fail to fulfil their responsibilities towards women.

Violence against women is never normal, legal or acceptable and should never be tolerated or justified. Everyone – individuals, communities, governments, and international bodies – has a responsibility to put a stop to it and to redress the suffering it causes.

Change must come at international, national and local levels. It must be brought about by governments as well as private actors, by institutions as well as individuals. International treaties must be respected, laws must be adopted or abolished, support systems must be put in place and above all attitudes, prejudices and social beliefs that foster and reinforce violence against women must change.

Preventing violence against women requires us to:

- Speak out against violence against women, listen to women and believe them;
- Condemn violence against women as the major human rights scandal of our times;
- Confront those in authority if they fail to prevent, punish and redress violence against women;
- Challenge religious, social, and cultural attitudes and stereotypes which diminish women's humanity;
- Promote women's equal access to political power, decision-making and resources; and
- Support women to organize themselves to stop the violence.

Amnesty International's worldwide campaign to Stop Violence against Women

Amnesty International will collaborate with women's rights activists and groups who are already working to expose and redress forms of violence. Amnesty International will investigate and expose acts of violence against women and demand that these violations are acknowledged, publicly condemned and redressed.

At the global level the Stop Violence against Women campaign:

- Calls on world leaders, organizations and individuals to publicly pledge to make the Universal Declaration of Human Rights – which promised equal rights and equal protection for all – a reality for all women.

Women from several women's groups in Manila, the Philippines, join forces in November 2002 to demand justice for victims of domestic violence ahead of a rally to commemorate the anniversary of the death of Maria Teresa Carlson. She was a former actress who had sought help after suffering years of domestic violence, and then apparently committed suicide by jumping from the 23rd floor of her apartment block.

At the international level the Stop Violence against Women campaign:

Urges all governments to:

- Ratify and implement the UN Convention on the Elimination of all Forms of Discrimination against Women and its Optional Protocol, without reservations.

- Ratify the Rome Statute of the International Criminal Court and adopt implementing national legislation to end impunity for violence against women in armed conflicts.

- Agree on an international Arms Trade Treaty to stop the proliferation of weapons used to commit violence against women.

Women demonstrate in Algiers on the eve of International Women's Day in March 2002 to demand the repeal of Algeria's family laws which discriminate against women.

Calls on UN and regional organizations to:

- Assist countries to develop action plans to end violence against women, and set up mechanisms to monitor their implementation.

- Fully and speedily implement UN Security Council Resolution 1325 on women, peace and security as well as the recommendations contained in the study by the UN Secretary-General on Women, Peace and Security.[149]

At the national level the Stop Violence against Women campaign:

- Demands the abolition of all laws that facilitate impunity for the rape or murder of women; criminalize consensual sexual relations in private; restrict a women's right to choose her partner; and restrict women's access to reproductive health care and family planning.

- Calls for laws to be adopted and enforced to protect women, to ensure that violence in the family is treated as seriously as assaults in other contexts, and that rape and other violence against women is criminalized.

- Calls on national and local authorities to fund and support measures to enable all women to live free from violence, such as programs of civic education, training and systems to support and protect victims of violence, and women's human rights defenders.

- Urges governments, financial institutions and corporate actors to counter women's impoverishment by ensuring equal access to economic and social rights, including food, water, property, employment and social entitlements and by safeguarding social safety nets, particularly in times of economic stress and dislocation.

"All are equal before the law and are entitled without any discrimination to equal protection of the law."
Universal Declaration of Human Rights

At the local level the Stop Violence against Women campaign:

- Urges communities to work to create an environment which supports women and addresses violence, by building community structures and processes to protect women, providing assistance to survivors of violence, raising awareness about violence against women, and ensuring that women human rights defenders are free to carry out their work.

- Demands that women be given equal access to decision-making in local government and community structures.

- Calls on religious bodies, traditional and informal authorities to denounce and desist from any action that encourages or tolerates violence against women, and respect women's human rights.

"Everyone has the right to take part in the government of [their] country, directly or through chosen representatives."
Universal Declaration of Human Rights

- Demands that armed groups make clear to their forces and supporters that violence against women is never acceptable, and that they discipline appropriately those under their command responsible for committing such acts. Where they exercise effective control over territory, armed groups must take measures to protect women from discrimination and violence and ensure that all perpetrators of violence against women are brought to justice.

- Urges every individual to challenge negative images of women and resist mass media, advertisements and school curriculums that reinforce discriminatory attitudes and perpetuate violence against women and girls.

- Calls on communities to work with those most affected by violence to develop and implement local strategies to confront violence against women.

"No one shall be subjected to torture or to cruel, inhuman or degrading treatment or punishment."
Universal Declaration of Human Rights

Appendix 1:

Selected Amnesty International reports on women's human rights

Mexico: Intolerable Killings – 10 Years of abductions and murder of women in Ciudad Juárez and Chihuahua (AI Index: AMR 41/026/2003)

Afghanistan: "No one listens to us and no one treats us as human beings" Justice denied to women (AI Index: ASA 11/023/2003)

United Kingdom: Decades of impunity – Serious allegations of rape of Kenyan women by UK Army Personnel (AI Index: EUR 45/014/2003)

Democratic Republic of Congo: Children at war (AI Index: AFR 62/034/2003)

Shattered Lives: The case for tough international arms control, published jointly with Oxfam (AI Index: ACT 30/001/2003)

Russia's hidden shame (AI Index: EUR 46/029/2003)

Kenya: Rape – the invisible crime (AI Index: AFR 32/001/2002)

Nigeria: BAOBAB for Women's Human Rights and Amnesty International – Joint statement on the implementation of new Sharia-based penal codes in northern Nigeria (AI Index: AFR 44/008/2002)

Protecting the human rights of women and girls: A medico-legal workshop on the care, treatment and forensic medical examination of rape survivors in Southern and East Africa (AI Index: AFR 53/001/2002)

Ecuador: Pride and Prejudice – Time to break the vicious circle of impunity for abuses against lesbian, gay, bisexual and transgendered people (AI Index: AMR 28/001/2002)

Guatemala: Guatemala's Lethal Legacy – Past Impunity and Renewed Human Rights Violations (AI Index: AMR 34/001/2002)

Pakistan: The Tribal Justice System (AI Index: ASA 33/024/2002)

Sri Lanka: Rape in custody (AI index: ASA 37/001/2002)

Spain: Crisis of identity – Race-related torture and ill-treatment by State Agents (AI Index: EUR 41/001/2002)

Claiming women's rights: the Optional Protocol to the UN Women's Convention (AI Index: IOR 51/08/2002)

"There is no excuse": Gender-based violence in the home and protection of the human rights of women in Spain AI Spain, November 2002; *No hay excusa. Violencia de género en el ámbito familiar y protección de los derechos humanos de las mujeres en España* AI España, Noviembre 2002

Liberia: Killings, torture and rape continue in Lofa County

(AI Index: AFR 34/009/2001)

India: The battle against fear and discrimination – The impact of violence against women in Uttar Pradesh and Rajasthan (AI Index: ASA 20/016/2001)

Myanmar: Torture of ethnic minority women (AI Index: ASA 16/017/2001)

Philippines: Fear, shame and impunity – Rape and sexual abuse of women in custody

(AI Index: ASA 35/001/2001)

Bangladesh: Attacks on members of the Hindu minority

(AI Index: ASA 13/006/2001)

Turkey: An end to torture and impunity is overdue! (AI Index: EUR 44/072/2001)

Lebanon: Torture and ill-treatment of women in pre-trial detention – a culture of acquiescence (AI Index: MDE 18/009/2001)

Broken Bodies, Shattered Minds. Torture and ill-treatment of women

(AI Index: ACT 40/001/2001)

Freedom from terror, safety from harm: challenge your government to stamp out the torture and ill-treatment of women (AI Index: ACT 77/002/2001)

Crimes of hate, conspiracy of silence: Torture and ill-treatment based on sexual identity

(AI Index: ACT 40/016/2001)

Investigating Women's Rights Violations in Armed Conflicts, Amnesty International Canada and International Centre for Human Rights and Democratic Development (ICHRDD), 2001

Sierra Leone: Rape and other forms of sexual violence against girls and women

(AI Index: AFR 51/035/2000)

Indonesia: The impact of impunity on women in Aceh (AI Index: ASA 21/060/2000)

Saudi Arabia: Gross human rights abuses against women

(AI Index: MDE 23/057/2000)

Israel: Human rights abuses of women trafficked from countries of the former Soviet Union into Israel's sex industry (AI Index: MDE 15/017/2000)

Respect, protect, fulfil – women's human rights: State responsibility for abuses by "non-state actors" (AI Index: IOR 50/001/2000)

International Criminal Court Fact Sheet 7: Ensuring justice for women
(AI Index: IOR 40/08/2000)

Monitoring and Investigating Sexual Violence. Amnesty International and Council for the Development of Social Science Research in Africa (CODESRIA), 2000

USA: "Not part of my sentence" – Violations of the human rights of women in custody
(AI Index: AMR 51/01/1999)

Women in Afghanistan: Pawns in men's power struggles (AI Index: ASA 11/11/1999)

Pakistan: Violence against women in the name of honour (AI Index: ASA 33/17/1999)

"The louder we will sing": Campaigning for lesbian and gay human rights
(AI Index: ACT 79/03/1999)

A Methodology for Gender-Sensitive Research, by Agnès Callamard, Amnesty International Canada and ICHRDD, 1999

Documenting Human Rights Violations by States Agents: Sexual Violence, by Agnès Callamard Amnesty International Canada and ICHRDD, 1999

What's in a word? (AI Index: ORG 33/02/1998)

1998: A Wonderful Year for Women's Human Rights? The United Nations, governments and the human rights of women (AI Index: IOR 40/12/1997)

Uganda: 'Breaking God's commands': the destruction of childhood by the Lord's Resistance Army (AI Index: AFR 59/01/1997)

Egypt: Women targeted by association (AI Index: MDE 12/011/1997)

Guatemala: Maquila workers among trade unionists targeted
(AI Index: AMR 34/028/1995)

Human rights are women's rights (AI Index: ACT 77/01/1995)

Bangladesh: Taking the law in their own hands – the village salish
(AI Index: ASA 13/12/1993)

Bosnia-Herzogovina: Rape and sexual abuse by armed forces
(AI Index: EUR 63/01/1993)

Women in the Front Line – Human rights violations against women
(AI Index: ACT 77/01/91)

Endnotes

1 "I kept the beatings secret for years", BBC news website, 14 February 2003; Jon Silverman, Domestic violence hits home, BBC news website, 28 May 2003.

2 Heise, L., Ellsberg, M. and Gottemoeller, M. *Ending Violence Against Women*. Population Reports, Series L, No. 11. Baltimore, Johns Hopkins University School of Public Health, December 1999, p. 1. (Hereafter Population Reports 11.)

3 Parliamentary Assembly of the Council of Europe, *Domestic Violence against Women*, Recommendation 1582. Adopted 27 September 2002.

4 See: UN Population Fund, 1999. *Violence Against Girls and Women: A Public Health Priority*, p.6.

5 Report of the Special Rapporteur on violence against women, its causes and consequences, 27 February 2003, UN Doc. E/CN.4/2003/75/Add.1, Addendum 1, International, regional and national developments in the area of violence against women, 1994-2003, para. 1494. (Hereafter UN SRVAW 2003.)

6 Fifth Periodic Report of the Russian Federation, UN Doc. CEDAW/C/USR/5, para. 6.

7 World Health Organization (WHO), Geneva, 2002. *World Report on Violence and Health*, p. 118. (Hereafter WHO 2002.)

8 CEDAW, General Recommendation No. 19, 1992, UN Doc. A/47/38, para. 6.

9 See the African Union's Protocol on the Rights of Women in Africa (July 2003), and the Council of Europe, Recommendation Rec(2002)5 of the Committee of Ministers to member states on the protection of women against violence, 30 April 2002.

10 *Traditional Culture Spreading HIV/AIDS*, UN Integrated Regional Information Networks, 28 March 2003.

11 Rodrick Mukumbira, "Shock treatment for widows as pandemic ravages Zimbabwe", *AFRICANEWS*, March 2002.

12 Rana Husseini, "Amman man gets 1 year for killing sister", *Jordan Times*, 1 June 2003.

13 Examples cited in "Gender and Small Arms", Wendy Cukier, Small Arms/Firearms Education and Research Network (SAFER-Net).

14 Testimony gathered by *Mesa de Trabajo: Mujer y Conflicto Armado*, in Medellín, Colombia.

15 Mayra Buvinic, Andrew Morrison and Michael Shifter, March 1999. *Violence in Latin America and the Caribbean: A Framework for Action*. Technical Study, Sustainable Development Department, Inter-American Development Bank, pp. 20-21.

16 Population Reports 11.

17 "When violence hits home", *Asahi Shimbun*, 8 July 2003.

18 World Bank, 1994, *A New Agenda for Women's Health and Nutrition*, p. 14.

19 *Domestic Violence in India 3: A Summary Report of a Multi-Site Household Survey*. International Center for Research on Women, 2000, Washington, DC, p. 32.

20 Mujeres Chilenas: Estadisticas para el Nuevo Siglo / Servicio Nacional de la Mujer, 2001.

21 "Sleeping with the enemy," *Barbados Daily Nation*, 20 July 2003.

22 Nikki Jecks, UNIFEM, 2002, *Ending Violence Against Women: Regional Scan for East and Southeast Asia*.

23 Cynthia Rothschild with Scott Long, *Written Out: How sexuality is used to attack women's organizing*, International Gay and Lesbian Human Rights Commission and the Center for Women's Global Leadership, 2000, p. 28.

24 Report of the Special Rapporteur on violence against women, UN Doc. E/CN.4/1997/47, 12 February 1997, para. 8. (Hereafter UN SRVAW 1997.)

25 WHO Draft working definition, October 2002.

26 Sangini (India) Trust, *Human Rights Report*, June 2003.

27 Cited in an interview in December 1994 by Bev Clark, author of *Lesbian Activism in Zimbabwe*.

28 Jonathan Kent, "Malaysian Minister: 'Lipstick invites rape'", 2 September 2003, BBC news website.

29 "Malaysian Minister in rape row", 9 October 2000, BBC news website.

30 University of Maine Rape Awareness Committee, Incidence and Prevalence, website.

31 Mike Earl-Taylor, "HIV/AIDS, the stats, the virgin cure and infant rape", *Science in Africa*, April 2002.

32 European Women's Lobby, 2001. *Persistence of gender inequalities – facts and figures in 1995-2000: Violence Against Women is a Most Common Crime.*

33 Women and Global Human Rights, Virginity testing, website.

34 Rosalind P. Petchesky, "Human Rights, Reproductive and Sexual Health and Economic Justice – Why they are Indivisible" in *Reproductive Health Matters*, Vol 8, No15, May 2000.

35 Alan Guttmacher Institute (AGI), "Hope and Realities" (1995), cited in Rebecca J. Cook and Bernard M. Dickens, "Human Rights Dynamics of Abortion Law Reform", in *Human Rights Quarterly*, Vol 25, 2003.

36 See the Protocol to the African Charter on Human and Peoples' Rights on the Rights of Women, Article 14, CEDAW General Recommendation No. 24; UN Doc. A/55/38, 2000, para. 180 (Jordan); UN Doc. A/55/38, 2000, (Myanmar) paras. 129-130; UN Doc. A/55/38/Rev.1, 1998, (Panama) para. 201; UN Doc. A/52/38/Rev.1, 1997, (Venezuela) para. 236.

37 CEDAW General Recommendation No. 24, Paragraph 31(c) "When possible, legislation criminalizing abortion could be amended, to remove punitive measures imposed on women who undergo abortion". The CEDAW Committee has asked states parties to review legislation making abortion illegal. See for example, Argentina, 23/07/97, UN Doc. A/52/38 Rev.1, Part II , para.319; Cameroon, 26/06/2000, UN Doc. A/55/38, para.60; Ireland, 01/07/99, UN Doc. A/54/38, para.186; Jordan, 27/01/2000, UN Doc. A/55/38, para.181; Nepal, 01/07/99, UN Doc. A/54/38, paras.139, 148.

In several sets of concluding observations, the Human Rights Committee has criticized legislation that criminalizes or severely restricts access to abortion. (See for example, Venezuela, 26/04/2001, UN Doc. CCPR/CO /71/V EN, para.19; Kuwait, 19/07/2000, UN Doc. CCPR/CO /69/KWT, A/55/40, para.15; Lesotho, 08/04/99, UN Doc. CCPR/C/79/Add.106, para.11) The Human Rights Committee has issued more specific recommendations to several states parties advising that they review or amend legislation criminalizing abortion. (See for example, Guatemala, 27/08/2001, UN Doc. CCPR/CO /72/G TM, para.19; Kuwait, 19/07/2000, UN Doc. CCPR/CO/69/KW T, A/55/40, para.16; Tanzania, 18/08/98, UN Doc. CCPR/C/79/Add.97, para.15.)

38 In light of these developments, Amnesty International is undergoing an internal consultation process with its membership to determine the circumstances under which, if ever, Amnesty International might support a woman's right to terminate a pregnancy.

39 Center for Reproductive Rights (formerly the Center for Reproductive Law and Policy), *Reproductive Rights 2000 Moving Forward*, Chapter 2, Part 1, p. 20.

40 UN Commission on Human Rights, The right of everyone to the enjoyment of the highest attainable standard of physical and mental health, UN Doc. E/CN.4/2003/L.32, 11 April 2003, para 6.

41 The Global Gag Rule Impact Project, 2003, Access Denied: U.S. Restrictions on International Family Planning.

42 Center for Reproductive Rights and Poradňa pre občianske a ludské práva (Center for Civil and Human Rights), *Body and Soul: Forced Sterilization and Other Assaults on Roma Reproductive Freedom in Slovakia*, New York, p. 60.

43 Report of the Special Rapporteur on violence against women, UN Doc. E/CN.4/1996/53, para. 27. (Hereafter UN SRVAW 1996.)

44 *State of Human Rights in 2002*, Human Rights Commission of Pakistan, 246-247.

45 Nafisa Shah, 1998. *A story in black: Karo kari killings in Upper Sindh*, Reuter Foundation Paper 100, Oxford, p. 5.

46 Worldwide it is estimated that well over 100 million women have been subjected to female genital mutilation.

47 *Female Genital Mutilation: An evaluation of the work of Amnesty International in four West African countries*, by Christine Naré (AI Index: AFR 01/004/2001)

48 Report of the Special Rapporteur on violence against women, UN Doc. E/CN.4/2002/83; 31 January 2002; para. 96. (Hereafter UN SRVAW 2002.)

49 Neferti Tadiar, 2000, quoted in INCITE! Women of Color Against Violence, website.

50 Citizen's Initiative, 2002, *How has the Gujarat massacre affected minority women? The survivors speak.* Fact-finding by a Women's Panel, p. 16.

51 UN SRVAW 2003, UN Doc. E/CN.4/2003/75, 6 January 2003, paras 61, 70.

52 *On the subject of race, gender and violence against women*, UN Doc. A/CONF. 189/PC.3/5, 27 July 2001, para 20.

53 John Stratton Hawley, 1999. "Fundamentalism", in Courtney W. Howland , ed., *Religious undamentalisms and the human rights of women*. St. Martin's Press, New York, p. 3.

54 Jennifer Butler, 'New Sheriff in Town': The Christian Right Shapes U.S. Agenda at the United Nations, in *The Public Eye*, Summer 2002: 14-21.

55 Joseph Ammu , "Women's rights at stake", *Hindustan Times*, 8 April 2003.

56 Talk given by Luz Marina Becerra in the Forum on the Situation of Displaced Populations in Soacha, organized by Bogotá Cómo Vamos, *El Tiempo*, Fundación Corona, October 2002.

57 Briefing paper on the 'feminisation of poverty'. Prepared by BRIDGE for the Swedish International Development Cooperation Agency (Sida). Report No 59, April 2001.

58 UNIFEM, "Dangerous Intersections: Violence Against Women and HIV/AIDS", Paper prepared for the 2001 World Conference against Racism in Durban, South Africa, 2001. (Hereafter, UNIFEM 2001.)

59 WHO 2002, p. 99.

60 UN SRVAW 1997, Add.3, para.36.

61 WHO, Division on Gender and Women's Health. *Violence Against women and HIV/AIDS: setting the research agenda*, Geneva, 2000.

62 UNAIDS, *Report on the global HIV/AIDS epidemic 2002*, pp. 62-69.

63 Wojcicki JM. "She drank his money": survival sex and the problem of violence in taverns in Gauteng province, South Africa. *Medical Anthropology Quarterly*. 2002 Sep;16(3):267-93.

64 WHO, Integrating Gender into HIV/AIDS Programmes, Expert consultation 3-5 June 2002, Geneva. p. 11.

65 Gregson S., "Disproportionate HIV infection of young girls linked to substantial age difference between female and male sexual partners", *The Lancet* 359: 1896, 2002.

66 UNAIDS, *Voluntary counselling and testing* (VCT), Geneva, May 2000.

67 See examples from Uganda in: Human Rights Watch, *Just Die Quietly: Domestic Violence and Women's Vulnerability to HIV in Uganda*, August 2003, Vol. 15, 15(A).

68 WHO, *Scaling up Antiretroviral Therapy in Resource-Limited Settings: Guidelines for a Public Health Approach*, Geneva 2002.

69 "Decision removes final patent obstacle to cheap drug imports", World Trade Organization, press release 350, 30 August 2003.

70 Joint NGO statement on TRIPS and public health, *WTO deal on medicines: a "gift" bound in red tape*, 10 September 2003.

71 Teixeira P.R., Vitoria M.A., Barcarolo J. "The Brazilian Experience in Providing Universal Access to Antiretroviral Therapy." In. J.P. Moati et. al. (eds.), *Economics of AIDS and Access to HIV/AIDS Care in Developing Countries. Issues and Challenges*. Paris: ANRS/National Agency for AIDS Research, 2003.

72 International Gay and Lesbian Human Rights Commission and Human Rights Watch, 2003. More than a Name, *State-sponsored Homophobia and Its Consequences in Southern Africa*, p. 176.

73 Belma Becirbasic and Dzenna Secic, *Invisible Casualties of War: Bosnia's raped women are being shunned by a society that refuses to see them as victims.*

74 Rose George, "Revolt against the Rapists", *The Guardian*, 5 April 2003.

75 Ruth Leger Sivard, *World Military and Social Expenditures 1991*. World Priorities Inc., USA.

76 *SIPRI Yearbook 2002*, Oxford University Press, Chapter 6, Military Expenditure.

77 Beijing Platform for Action, Strategic Objective E2, para. 143b.

78 Quoted in Bhaskar Menon, *Small arms and Light Weapons and the United Nations*, The NGO Committee on Disarmament, Peace and Security; UN Doc A/52/298, 1997.

79 *Small Arms Survey 2002*, Graduate Institute of International Studies, Geneva.

80 Commission on Reception, Truth and Reconciliation in Timor-Leste (CAVR), *National Public Hearing on Women and Conflict*, CAVR National Headquarters, former Comarca Balide, Dili, 28-29 April 2003.

81 Report of the Special Rapporteur on violence against women, Addendum: Report on the mission to Haiti, E/CN.4/2000/68/Add.3, 2000, para. 58.

82 "Domestic violence against Palestinian women rises," *Middle East Times*, 20 September 2002, based on reporting from Agence France-Presse.

83 Cited in Jon Ellison and Catherine Lutz, "Hidden Casualties," *Southern Exposure*, 15 May 2003.

84 WHO 2002, p. 15.

85 See *Shattered Lives: The Case for Tough International Arms Controls*, Amnesty International and Oxfam International, October 2003 (AI Index: ACT 30/003/2003).

86 Medica Zenica 1999, in Cheywa Spindel, Elisa Levy, Melissa Connor,.2000, *With An End in Sight: Strategies from the UNIFEM Trust Fund to Eliminate Violence Against Women*. UNIFEM, p. 89.

87 Julie Poucher Harbin, "Families at war," *Institute for War and Peace Reporting*, 5 September 2001.

88 Human Rights Watch, *Hopes Betrayed: Trafficking of Women and Girls to Post-Conflict Bosnia and Herzegovina for Forced Prostitution*, November 2002.

89 Elisabeth Rehn and Ellen Johnson Sirleaf, 2002. "Women War Peace: The Independent Experts' Assessment", Progress of the World's Women 2002, Vol. 1, UNIFEM, p. 40.

90 Nicole Itano, "3,000 Rwanda Women Await Trials for Genocide" *Women's Enews*, 12 December 2002.

91 Coalition to stop the use of child soldiers, 2000. *Girls with Guns: An Agenda on Child Soldiers for "Beijing Plus Five"*.

92 Cited in *Mesa de Trabajo: Mujer y Conflict Armado*, "Informe Sobre Violencia Sociopolítica contra Mujeres y Niñas en Colombia," Bogotá, February 2003.

93 UN SRVAW 2002, Add.3, para. 52.

94 Testimony to the *Comité Andino de Servicios*, Bogotá, Colombia, July 2001.

95 Testimony to the *Comité Andino de Servicios*, Bogotá, Colombia, July 2001.

96 *Héritiers de la Justice*, a non-governmental organization working in eastern Democratic Republic of the Congo.

97 Women's Commission for Refugee Women and Children, 1998. *Forgotten Prisoners: A follow-up report on refugee women incarcerated in York County, PA*, p. 7.

98 Preamble, UN Charter.

99 A general recommendation or general comment to a treaty provides a fuller analysis and interpretation of the articles of the treaty in question, and is considered expert jurisprudence of international human rights law.

100 Important milestones in the 1990s were the World Conference on Human Rights (Vienna, 1993); the International Conference on Population and Development (Cairo, 1994); the World Summit on Social Development (Copenhagen, 1995); the Fourth World Conference on Women (Beijing, 1995); Beijing plus five (New York, 2000); UN Special Session on HIV/AIDS (New York, 2003).

101 For example, the definition of rape refers to "invasion of the body" "committed by force, threat of force or coercion, such as that caused by fear of violence, duress, detention, psychological oppression, or abuse of power... or the person was incapable of giving genuine consent (including age-related incapacity)". Draft Elements of Crimes, UN Doc. PCNICC/2000/1/Add.2.

102 Adopted by the General Assembly of the Organization of American States in June 1994.

103 Case 12.051, Report No. 54/01, Maria da Penha Maia Fernandes, (Brazil).

104 Human Rights Committee, General Comment 28, Equality of rights between men and women (article 3), UN Doc. CCPR/C/21/Rev.1/Add.10 (2000).

105 Article 19, Vienna Convention on the Law of Treaties.

106 M. McPhedran, S. Bazilli, M. Erickson, A. Byrnes, *The First CEDAW Impact Study, Final Report*, International Women's Rights Project and Centre for Feminist Research, York University, 2000. (Hereafter The First CEDAW Impact Study.)

107 A leading case defining the doctrine of due diligence is *Velásquez Rodríguez*, Judgment of 29 July 1988, Inter-American Court of Human Rights, Series C, no. 4, paras. 174-5.

108 AI Index: ACT 40/001/2001.

109 AI Index: ACT 40/016/2001.

110 Delic, Delalic, Mucic and Landzo, IT-96-21-T.

111 Kunarac, Kovac and Vukovic IT-96-23 and IT-96-23/1.

112 One key recent case reaffirming this principle was UK House of Lords in *Islam v. Secretary of State for the Home Department Regina v. Immigration Appeal Tribunal and Another, Ex parte Shah* [1999] UKHL 20 (25 March, 1999).

113 INCITE! Women of Color Against Violence. *"Violence Against Women of Color"* , website, 24 April 2003.

114 Nikki Jecks, UNIFEM, 2002, *Ending Violence Against Women: Regional Scan for East and Southeast Asia*, p. 7.

115 UN SRVAW 2003, para. 766.

116 Center for Reproductive Law and Policy and the *Estudio para la Defensa de los Derechos de la Mujer* (DEMUS), 2000. *Women of the World: Law and Policies Affecting their Reproductive Lives – Latin American and the Caribbean, Progress Report 2000.* New York p.14.

117 UN SRVAW 2003, para. 726.

118 UN SRVAW 2003, para. 256.

119 *Early Marriage in a Human Rights Context*, Background prepared for the 10 May 2002 UN General Assembly Special Session on Children.

120 UNMIK Regulation 2001/4, *The Prohibition of Trafficking in Persons in Kosovo*, 12 January 2001. Further, as a short-term measure, a Memorandum of Agreement between the OSCE and UNMIK established an Interim Security Facility which opened on 16 June 2003 for one year "to protect and support victims of trafficking." OSCE Mission, 5th report, May 2003.

121 UNMIK Regulation 2001/4: Section 4.1.

122 Janice Du Mont, "No magic bullet: findings from a three-stage evaluation of the collection of medico-legal evidence in sexual assault cases." Presentation to the Medical Research Council of South Africa Conference on Gender Based Violence and Health, Johannesburg, South Africa, 7-9 May 2003.

123 Associated Press, "Bill for evidence collection increases the trauma of rape, victim says", 10 February 2003.

124 FIDA (K), 1997. *Second Class Citizenship*, Annual Report for 1996-1997.

125 This term, meaning "oppressed", is widely used to describe members of the "Scheduled Castes", formerly referred to as "Untouchables".

126 Submission on behalf of Anti-Slavery International, the Indonesian Migrant Workers' Union and the Asian Migrant Centre to the UN Sub-Commission on the Promotion and Protection of Human Rights, Working Group on Contemporary Forms of Slavery, 16 - 20 June 2003.

127 Interview with Shawna Virago, Community United Against Violence, in *Whose Safety? Women of Color and the Violence of Law Enforcement*, co-published by the American Friends Service Committee and Committee on Women, Population and the Environment, 2001, by Annanya Bhattacharjee, p. 35.

128 National Coalition of Anti-Violence Programs, 1999. *Anti-Lesbian, Gay, Bisexual and Transgender Violence in 1998."* Quoted in Bhattacharjee, op. cit, pp. 35-36.

129 *Jerusalem Post*, "Unchain their hearts," 1 March 1999.

130 Human Rights Watch, 2003. *Double Standards: Women's Property Rights Violations in Kenya*, Vol. 15, No. 5, p. 11.

131 Report of the National Committee on Political Tribalism, chaired by Hon. Justice James Kerr, O.J.Q.C., Political Ombudsman, 1997, paras 32-3.

132 Caroline Turrif, "Rape, sexual abuse of girls said at record levels, source of soaring HIV infection rate." *Sunday Observer*, 1 December 2002.

133 Op. cit.

134 Testimony of two public officials cited in *Mesa de Trabajo: Mujer y Conflict Armado*, "Informe Sobre Violencia Sociopolítica contra Mujeres, Jóvenes y Niñas en Colombia," Bogotá, February 2003.

135 UN Doc. A/CONF.121/22/Rev.1 at 59 (1985).

136 *Pakistan: The Tribal Justice System* (AI Index: ASA 33/024/2002).

137 Action India, organizational material and personal communication, 2002.

138 Shramajibee Mahila Samity, "Shalishi in West Bengal: A Community-Based Response to Domestic Violence" *Economic and Political Weekly*, April 26-May 2, 2003, pp.1665-1673.

139 WHO 2002, footnote 73, p. 176.

140 Extracted from Cheywa Spindel, Elisa Levy and Melissa Connor, 2000, *With An End in Sight: Strategies from the UNIFEM Trust Fund to Eliminate Violence Against Women.* NY: UNIFEM. (Hereafter UNIFEM 2000.)

141 Susana T. Fried, "Violence Against Women", in *Health and Human Rights: An International Journal.* Vol. 6, No. 2, 2003, pp. 88-111.

142 George Hicks, 1995, *The Comfort Women: Japan's Brutal Regime of Enforced Prostitution in the Second World War*, W. W. Norton. W. W. Norton & Company, Incorporated, 1995.

143 International Center for Research on Women and The Centre for Development and Population Activities, Washington DC, USA, 1999.

144 Elizabeth Guerrero-Caviedes, *Violence Against Women in Latin America and the Caribbean 1990-2000: An Assessment of a Decade*, 2002, UNIFEM Regional Office of Latin America and the Caribbean and Isis International, Santiago de Chile.

145 The First CEDAW Impact Study.

146 UN SRVAW 2003, para. 1432.

147 UNIFEM 2000.

148 Queen Sophia Centre, Valencia, Spain, Database on violence against women.

149 Queen Sophia Centre, Valencia, Spain, Database on violence against women.

150 UN Security Council Resolution 1325 invited the Secretary-General to carry out a study on the impact of armed conflict on women and girls.